INTERNATIONAL AND COMPARATIVE CRIMINAL LAW SERIES

REDRESSING MISCARRIAGES OF JUSTICE

Practice and Procedure in National and International Criminal Law Cases

GEERT-JAN ALEXANDER KNOOPS

Transnational Publishers

Sdu Uitgevers

Published and distributed by
Transnational Publishers, Inc.
410 Saw Mill River Road
Ardsley, NY 10502

Phone: 914-693-5100
Fax: 914-693-4430
E-mail: info@transnationalpubs.com
Web: www.transnationalpubs.com

For sales in the Benelux (Belgium, Netherlands and Luxemburg) only:
Sdu Klantenservice
Postbus 20014
2500 EA Den Haag

Phone: (070) 37 89 880
Fax: (070) 37 89 783
Email: klantenservice@sdu.nl
Web: www.sdu.nl

Library of Congress Cataloging-in-Publication Data

Knoops, Geert-Jan G. J.

Redressing miscarriages of justice : practice and procedure in national and international criminal law / Geert-Jan Alexander Knoops.
p. cm.—(International and comparative criminal law series)
Includes bibliographical references and index.
1. Judicial error. I. Title.

K5560.K59 2006 345'.01—dc22

2006044689

Transnational ISBN: 1-57105-368-9
Sdu Uitgevers ISBN: 9012115809

Manufactured in the United States of America

TABLE OF CONTENTS

PREFACE

With the advent and refinement of forensic sciences in the last two decades, miscarriages of justice as societal and legal phenomena, as well as facts of judicial life, have become more visible and prominent. Although this is especially true in capital cases in the United States, numerous miscarriages of justice have also occurred in Europe. Analysis of such erroneous convictions provides a window through which one can observe the (in)fallibility and inherent deficiencies of criminal justice systems. "Convicting the innocent shows the fallibility of every other decision made by politicians and criminal justice personnel. It shows they make godlike decisions without godlike skills."[1]

This book aims at providing an insight into both the procedural and substantive legal aspects of the prevention, as well as the redressing of miscarriages of justice. Such analysis is inextricably connected with delving deeper into contemporary developments within forensic science. The complexity of the forensic sciences and their transposition onto international criminal procedure is still an underdeveloped area. This issue is extensively dealt with below in Chapter 8.

The promulgation of legal and practical standards for the review of criminal cases is of perennial concern. Defense lawyers, facing potential miscarriages of justice, are often confronted with ambiguous legal review standards in criminal law codes. Building on analysis of standards in various criminal law systems, as well as those within the statutes of international and internationalized criminal tribunals, this book provides an overview of the subject and is intended to serve as a textbook for practitioners, while simultaneously formulating guidelines on how to proceed in these type of cases and adjudicate them.

Practitioners specializing in the complex area of redressing miscarriages of justice by way of review procedures are rare. Doughty Street

---

1 *See* Michael L. Radelet, *Foreword, in* WRONGLY CONVICTED: PERSPECTIVES ON FAILED JUSTICE xi (Saundra D. Westervelt & John A. Humphrey eds., 2001).

Chambers, London, is one of the prominent offices in common law that prides itself on this expertise. Knoops & Partners Lawyers, Amsterdam, the firm to which I belong, has dealt with a number of landmark cases in this area within the civil law jurisdictions. However, an important task and responsibility for advocacy lies ahead—to grow in knowledge and familiarity with the procedural complexity of review procedures. The acquisition of such knowledge is sure to be beneficial in seeking prevention of miscarriages of justice.

In thanking those who have assisted in the preparation of this study, I recall those who have contributed to the development of my academic career and, in particular, my legal partner and wife, Carry Juliette Hamburger, for her substantive contribution to this study as well as her moral support. In addition, I am grateful to the members of my law office, Knoops & Partners Lawyers, for their trust in me. In particular, I am indebted to Janneke Boumans, who assisted me in researching materials for this book, and to Frederique Wessel for her extensive work on the manuscript. I am indebted to my loyal friend Wayne Jordash, barrister at Doughty Street Chambers, London, for his intellectual inspiration and trust.

I am also grateful to a former student of mine, Niels van Schaik, whose thesis was dedicated to the subject of miscarriages of justice in the Netherlands and formed an important source for British case law on the subject. Finally, I am once again indebted to my publisher, Heike Fenton, and my editor, Terence Hegarty, for their confidence and encouragement.

The law in this book is stated as of February 16, 2006.

ABOUT THE AUTHOR

Geert-Jan Alexander Knoops (b.1960) is a Professor of international criminal law at Utrecht University. He also practices international criminal law and extradition law at Knoops and Partners Lawyers, Amsterdam, and has appeared and appears as defense counsel before several international fora such as the European Court of Human Rights in Strasburg, the ICTR, ICTY, and Special Court for Sierra Leone. Currently he is acting lead counsel before the ICTY and the Special Court for Sierra Leone. Knoops is also admitted as defense counsel to the bar of the International Criminal Court at the Hague. His academic books include *Defenses in Contemporary International Criminal Law* (2001), *Surrendering to International Criminal Courts: Contemporary Practice and Procedure* (2002), *An Introduction to the Law of International Criminal Tribunals: A Comparative Study* (2003), and *Theory and Practice of International and Inernationalized Criminal Proceedings* (2005). His doctoral dissertation of 1998 titled *"Duress and law-finding"* (Leiden University) relates to a comparative study on the international criminal law defense of duress and the mental dimension of this defense. He was awarded a second Ph.D. degree in international law on October 11, 2004, at the National University of Ireland, which thesis is titled: *The Prosecution and Defense of Peacekeepers under International Criminal Law*. Knoops holds the rank of major (reserve) in the Royal Netherlands Marines Corps and was assigned as military legal advisor in several international military exercises.

LIST ABBREVIATIONS

ACHR	American Convention on Human Rights
AFRC	Armed Forces Revolutionary Council
AJIL	American Journal of International Law
ALL ER	All England Reports
CACD	Court of Appeal Criminal Division
CCRC	(British) Criminal Cases Review Commission
CDF	civilian defense forces
DNA	deoxyribo nucleic acid
Doc.	Document
DPP	Department of the Public Prosecutor
EC	Euopean Community
ECHR	European Court of Human Rights
EJIL	European Journal of International Law
et al.	and others
FBI	Federal Bureau of Investigation
FRE	Federal Rules of Evidence (U.S.)
FSS	British Forensic Sciences Services
IACHR	Inter-American Commission on Human Rights
ICC Statute	Rome Statute of the International Criminal Court, A/Conf. 183/9, July 17, 1998
ICC	International Criminal Court
ICCPR	International Covenant on Civil and Political Rights
ICJ	International Court of Justice
ICTR	International Criminal Tribunal for Rwanda
ICTY	International Criminal Tribunal for the Former Yugoslavia
Id.	Idem ("same")
ILC	International Law Commission
IPA	Innocence Protection Act
IRA	Irish Republican Army
JICJ	Journal of International Criminal Justice
KRT	Khmer Rouge Tribunal

LCN	low copy number method
LR	Likelihood ratio
mRNA	messenger RNA
mtDNA	mitochondrial DNA testing
NG	nitroglycerine
OTP	office of the prosecution
paras.	paragraphs
PCR	polymerase chain reaction method
RNA	ribo nucleic acid
RFLP	restriction fragment length polymorphism technique
RPE	Rules of Procedure and Evidence
RUF	Revolutionary United Front
R	Regina
SCSL	Special Court for Sierra Leone
STRs	short tandem repeats
Supp.	Supplement
UNHRC	United Nations Human Rights Committee
v.	versus
Vols.	Volumes

CHAPTER 1

THE NEED FOR EFFECTIVE RETRIAL PROCEDURES IN INTERNATIONAL CRIMINAL CASES

A. WRONGFUL CONVICTIONS AND THEIR INTER-RELATIONSHIP WITH THE NATURE OF THE CRIMINAL JUSTICE SYSTEM

The judicial process in criminal cases does not require a mathematical exercise. In civil law or inquisitorial systems, it depends largely on the compilation of a file, the "dossier," while within common law or adversarial systems it depends largely on the outcome of examination and cross-examination of witnesses at trial. To put it differently, the common law system may be seen as "party-driven," as the parties themselves drive the case forward and the judge is merely an umpire. When the trial starts, there is no evidence before the judge; the parties themselves are responsible for the submission of evidence. The civil law system, however, may be seen as "judge-driven"; the trial judge plays the leading role at trial, which extends to the examination of witnesses. The trial judge does so on the basis of the "dossier," which is prepared by the investigating judge or prosecutor.[1] As a consequence, there may be instances in which the judiciary lacks complete insight into all the relevant facts that are determinative for achieving justice. In both the civil law "dossier" approach and the common law adversarial approach, it may happen that not all facts are adduced to the criminal law judge.

Moreover, and perhaps inevitably, new facts may come up after a criminal trial has been concluded and become irreversible. Such situations may result in criminal convictions that are unsafe or even qualify as miscarriages of justice. Here, a distinction should be drawn between

[1] *See* RICHARD MAY & MARIEKE WIERDA, INTERNATIONAL CRIMINAL EVIDENCE 17 (2002).

a wrongful conviction and a miscarriage of justice. Whereas wrongful convictions do not necessarily imply that, objectively speaking, the wrongfully convicted is innocent, the term "miscarriage of justice" is associated with an innocent convicted person. Yet the term "miscarriage of justice" is sometimes also canvassed in a broader sense, namely as encompassing cases that resulted in retrial without factual innocence being proven. Miscarriages of justice, understood in this broad sense, may thus encompass several categories of cases. Gudjonsson identifies four of these:

> (1) A miscarriage may occur because the defendant did not receive a fair trial, even though he may have committed the offense in question. Therefore, the defendant may be *legally innocent*, but *factually guilty*. For example, a defendant who is convicted on the basis of fabricated evidence, even though he committed the offense, is innocent in law, as he was convicted by unfair means and in violation of due legal process.
>
> (2) A defendant who was only marginally involved in the case may be convicted of a more serious charge.
>
> (3) The wrong person may be convicted for the offense committed.
>
> (4) The alleged crime for which the defendant was convicted may in fact never have been committed. In other words, the *actus reus* of the alleged offense has not been correctly established.[2]

When one regards this subject from the viewpoint of the doctrine of *error facti*—meaning that one mistakenly believes the absence or presence of a particular fact that is causative for a certain criminal law judgment—the term "miscarriage of justice" would embrace such a broad interpretation. The doctrine of *error facti* features within the system of criminal law defenses and could, by way of analogy, be of assistance in the clarification of the analysis of miscarriages of justice.

---

2 GISLI H. GUDJONSSON, THE PSYCHOLOGY OF INTERROGATIONS, CONFESSIONS AND TESTIMONY 206 (1993).

B. EFFECTIVE RETRIAL OR REVIEW PROCEDURES: PROTECTION OF THE INTEGRITY OF CRIMINAL TRIALS

In most criminal cases that lead to a retrial, the actual perpetrator is not detected. Yet, in these instances, the conviction can still turn out to be unsafe.

The legitimacy of a criminal justice system is based largely upon both its effectiveness and its fairness. Its effectiveness is determined by its ability to investigate and detect crime, identify offenders, and impose the appropriate sanctions on those who have been convicted of offenses. Its fairness is judged by its thoroughness and the efforts it requires to redress the resource imbalance between the accused and the state at the investigatory, pre-trial, trial, and appellate stages. The system should do this by providing evidentiary protection and effective legal representation at all points.

Wrongful convictions undermine both prongs of the criminal justice system's legitimacy:

(1) If someone is wrongfully convicted, that person is punished for an offense he or she did not commit, and the actual perpetrator of the crime goes free.

(2) Public confidence in the system declines when wrongful convictions are identified.

The criminal justice system is based on the fundamental legal value that an accused is legally presumed innocent until proven guilty. This may contradict the public expectation that most of those charged with criminal offenses are, and will be found to be, guilty. Wrongful convictions undermine both this fundamental legal value and this public expectation, since they show that the presumption of innocence may be honored in its breach and that the criminal justice system does not only deal with the guilty.

Public attention has been brought to the issue of wrongful convictions by, for instance, the Canadian case against Donald Marshall[3] and

---

[3] *See* Royal Commission on the Donald Marshall Jr. Prosecution, N.S.R.2d, Dec. 1989.

the Rubin "Hurricane" Carter case in the United States.[4] As to the frequency of wrongful conviction cases, it has been claimed that in Great Britain, the wrongful conviction rate may be as high as 0.1 percent, or one out of every thousand convictions. Another estimate is that there may be 15 cases of wrongful convictions each year in Great Britain. Academic studies in the United States indicate that between 0.5 and 1 percent of persons convicted of serious offenses did not commit the crime. It has also been suggested by the Criminal Justice Research Center that as many as 6,000 persons a year are wrongfully convicted of felonies in the United States. Although there are no similar estimates of the number of wrongful convictions in Canada, it is estimated that the Canadian Department of Justice receives about 30 applications a year for the review of criminal convictions.[5] Because findings of wrongful conviction represent a basic undermining of the integrity of the criminal justice system, effective procedures for the review of such cases are of perennial importance. Yet law practice shows that existing procedures are rarely invoked successfully. This book focuses on the effectiveness of these review procedures and on the question of whether review remedies should be expanded.

---

[4] *See* Chapter 3.

[5] *See* Jim Middlemiss, *Guilty Until Proven Innocent*, 3 CANADIAN LAW. 20–25 (1991).

CHAPTER 2

PROTECTION AGAINST MISCARRIAGES OF JUSTICE WITHIN INTERNATIONAL CRIMINAL LAW: AN *ERGA OMNES* OBLIGATION

A. INTRODUCTION: THE APPLICABILITY OF THE DOCTRINE OF STATE RESPONSIBILITIES *ERGA OMNES*

One of the most important problems of contemporary criminal law, both national and international, is to identify a potential miscarriage of justice in a timely way and to protect the affected legal community from it. The emergence of international and internal armed conflicts and terrorism threats have increasingly pressured states to adopt new laws to suppress international and transnational crimes and have led police and judicial authorities to conduct arrests in order to deter others who potentially have criminal intentions. These contemporary international law enforcement emergencies present a grave dilemma—that of overcoming an emergency and restoring legal order in states while at the same time respecting the fundamental rights of individuals. These developments increase the risk of wrongly detained and convicted persons. To what extent do states themselves bear the legal obligation and responsibility of preventing and redressing miscarriages of justice?

This question is highly relevant. During the last decade, due to new insights, numerous miscarriages of justice in capital cases have been identified. In this regard, the words of U.S. Senator Patrick Leahy, introducing the Innocence Protection Act of 2001 in the United States of America,[1] underline the responsibilities of states in this regard:

> It seems like every time you pick up a paper these days, there is another story about another person who was sentenced to death

---

1 This act will be discussed in Section B.

> for a crime that he did not commit. The most horrifying miscarriages of justice are becoming commonplace: "Yet another Innocent Person Cleared By DNA, Walks Off Death Row"—story on page 10. We should never forget that behind each of these headlines is a person whose life was completely shattered and nearly extinguished by a wrongful conviction.
>
> And those were the "lucky" ones. We simply do not know how many innocent people remain on death row, and how many may already have been executed.
>
> People of good conscience can and will disagree on the morality of the death penalty. I have always opposed it. I did when I was a prosecutor, and I do today. But no matter what you believe about the death penalty, no one wants to see innocent people sentenced to death. It is completely unacceptable.[2]

In many wrongful conviction cases, states, using the societal need and interest to prosecute grave crimes as an excuse, have denied the application of fundamental standards of due process, including denial of a criminal prosecution and trial that ensures disclosure of both exculpatory and inculpatory evidence and access thereto for the defense on a footing equal to that of the prosecution. The "complete unacceptability" of convicting innocent people, as formulated by U.S. Senator Leahy, raises the question of whether redressing miscarriages of justice is merely a matter of the parties in a criminal case or involves state responsibilities as such. In particular, it is legitimate to ask whether reversing miscarriages of justice amounts to an obligation *erga omnes* under international law, in that the observance of this responsibility serves a community interest.

The doctrine of obligations *erga omnes* was developed by the International Court of Justice (ICJ) in the 1970 *Barcelona Traction* case, in which the ICJ, with reference to the obligation of a state concerning the treatment of aliens in its territory, held that:

> These obligations . . . are neither absolute nor unqualified. In particular, an essential distinction should be drawn between the

---

2 *See* Senator Leahy's Remarks on the Introduction of the Innocence Protection Act of 2001, *reprinted in* 29 HOFSTRA L. REV. 1114, 1113–17 (2001).

> obligations of a state towards the international community as a whole, and those arising vis-à-vis another state in the field of diplomatic protection. By their very nature the former are the concern of all states. In view of the importance of the rights involved, all states can be held to have a legal interest in their protection; they are obligations *erga omnes*.[3]

Importantly, the ICJ clarified the essential distinction between obligations *erga omnes* and other obligations of international law as follows:

> Obligations the performance of which is the subject of diplomatic protection are not of the same category. It cannot be held, when one such obligation in particular is in question, in a specific case, that all states have a legal interest in its observance. In order to bring a claim in respect of the breach of such an obligation, a state must first establish its right to do so.[4]

The question merits thought as to whether redressing miscarriages of justice falls within the purview of state obligations *erga omnes*. An affirmative answer may be derived from the following arguments:

First, in the *Barcelona Traction* case the Court gave some indication as to which obligations "by their very nature" qualified as obligations *erga omnes*. In contemporary international law, such obligations derive, for example, from the outlawing of acts of aggression and of genocide, and from the principles and rules concerning the basic rights of the human person, including protection from slavery and racial discrimination.[5] Notably, the ICJ adds that "some of the contemporary rights of protection have entered into the body of general international law; others are conferred by international instruments of a universal or quasi-universal character."[6] It is tenable that protection against miscarriages of justice qualifies as such a "basic right of the human person," which has "entered into the body of general international law." This interpretation is reinforced by the ICJ judgment in the *Barcelona Traction* case where the Court says that "with regard more particularly to human rights

---

3 *See* Barcelona Traction (Light and Power Co. Case), 1970 I.C.J. 3, at 32.

4 *Id.*

5 *Id.*

6 *Id.*

. . . it should be noted that these also include protection against denial of justice."[7]

It is certainly the case that protection against denial of justice enhances protection against miscarriages of justice.

Second, it should be observed that the ICJ's judgment does not make clear whether "basic rights of the human person," which give rise to obligations *erga omnes*, are equivalent to human rights *tout court*, or are limited to those relating to the human person and human dignity. Yet it is arguable that, based on the criteria for qualifying human right norms as *erga omnes* obligations, as set out by Ragazzi,[8] protection against miscarriages of justice falls within this category. Ragazzi puts forward five criteria for identifying obligations *erga omnes* based on the examples given in the *Barcelona Traction* case. First, all four examples relate to narrowly defined obligations. Second, all the examples are essentially those of negative obligations. Third, all the examples are those of obligations or duties in the strict sense (i.e., what one ought or ought not to do). Fourth, all the examples are those of obligations deriving from rules of general international law belonging to *jus cogens* and codified by international treaties to which a high number of states have become parties. Finally, all the examples are those of obligations "instrumental to the main political objectives of the present time, namely, the preservation of peace and the promotion of fundamental human rights, which in turn reflect basic goods (or moral values), first and foremost life and human dignity." Ragazzi describes this list as descriptive rather than prescriptive. This author goes on to examine the scope of potential obligations inherent in the category of obligations *erga omnes*, thus enlarging the concept to include general principles (in relation to human rights law), positive obligations (in relation to development law), and obligations attaching to optional rights (in relation to environmental law).[9]

From this perspective, protection against miscarriages of justice falls within the ambit of states obligation *erga omnes*. After all, as the work of Gudjonsson indicates, criminal justice systems themselves are "defi-

---

7 *Id.*, para. 47.

8 *See* M. Ragazzi, The Concept of International Obligations *Erga Omnes* 132–34 (1997).

9 *Id.* at 132–63.

cient in discovering, admitting to, and doing something about, errors which they make."[10]

The next two sections will develop additional arguments in support of this conclusion.

B. THE GENESIS OF THE *ERGA OMNES* DOCTRINE: THE U.S. INNOCENCE PROTECTION ACT

These developments and this growing consciousness resulted on October 30, 2004, in the United States in the signing into law of the Innocence Protection Act (IPA) as part of the larger Justice for All Act, a comprehensive piece of legislation.[11]

> The bill passed the U.S. Senate by voice vote on October 9, 2004 and the U.S. House of Representatives on October 6, 2004 in an overwhelming 393-14 vote. This omnibus legislation enhances the rights and protections for all persons involved in the criminal justice system through two different, but complementary mechanisms: (1) a new set of statutory victims' rights that are both enforceable in a court of law and supported by fully-funded victims' assistance programs and (2) a comprehensive DNA bill that seeks to ensure that the true offender is caught and convicted for the crime.[12]

Importantly, the U.S. President, who signed this bill, acknowledged the need for expanded DNA testing and better legal representation to help prevent wrongful convictions.[13]

The Innocence Protection Act, which is part of the Justice for All Act of 2004,[14] is a carefully crafted package of criminal justice reforms aimed at reducing the risk that innocent persons may be convicted. Most

---

[10] G.H. Gudjonsson, The Psychology of Interrogations and Confessions: A Handbook (2003).

[11] *See* Justice for All Act of 2004 (Incorporating Innocence Protection Act of 2001–S. 486), Pub. L. No. 108-405, 108th Cong., 2d Sess. (2004).

[12] *See The Justice Project Campaign for Criminal Justice Reform* (Nov. 2004), *at* www.CJReform.org.

[13] *Id.*

[14] *See supra* note 11.

urgently, the law affords greater access to DNA testing for convicted offenders, and helps states to improve the quality of legal representation in capital cases. This important law provides critical new safeguards in capital cases by:

(1) ensuring convicted offenders the right to request DNA testing on evidence that is in the government's possession;

(2) helping states provide professional and experienced legal assistance at every stage of a death penalty case; and

(3) providing those who are proven innocent, after an unjust incarceration, some measure of compensation.

In order to analyze the ramifications of this development for international and national criminal trials, it is instructive to review the factual and legal findings of the U.S. Congress that underlie the 2001 Innocence Protection Act. In Section 101, titled "Findings and Purposes," pertaining to said bill, the following paragraphs shed an important light on the topicality of wrongful convictions in criminal law:

(4) Since DNA testing is often feasible on relevant biological material that is decades old, it can, in some circumstances, prove that a conviction that predated the development of DNA testing was based upon incorrect factual findings. Uniquely, DNA evidence showing innocence, produced decades after a conviction, provides a more reliable basis for establishing a correct verdict than any evidence proffered at the original trial. DNA testing therefore, can and has resulted in the post-conviction exoneration of innocent men and women.

(5) In more than 80 cases in the United States, DNA evidence has led to the exoneration of innocent men and women who were wrongfully convicted. This number includes at least 10 individuals sentenced to death, some of who came within days of being executed.

(6) In more than a dozen cases, post-conviction DNA testing that has exonerated an innocent person has also enhanced

> public safety by providing evidence that led to the identification of the actual perpetrator.[15]

As a result, Section 102 of this bill empowers courts to order "DNA testing if it has the scientific potential to produce new exculpatory evidence material to the inmate's claim of innocence. When the test results are exculpatory, courts shall order a hearing and make such further orders as may be appropriate under existing law." Section 102 prohibits the destruction of biological evidence in a criminal case while a defendant remains incarcerated, absent prior notification to such defendant of the government's intent to destroy the evidence."[16]

As to the legal-political considerations that underlie this shift towards a more pertinent governmental acknowledgement that miscarriages of justice happen and governments bear responsibility to prevent and redress them, it is relevant to take notice of findings 14–16 of the U.S. Congress, which introduce this bill:

> (14) It shocks the conscience and offends social standards of fairness and decency to execute innocent persons or to deny inmates the opportunity to present persuasive evidence of their innocence.
>
> (15) If biological material is not subjected to DNA testing in appropriate cases, there is a significant risk that persuasive evidence of innocence will not be detected and, accordingly, that innocent persons will be unconstitutionally executed.
>
> (16) Given the irremediable constitutional harm that would result from the execution of an innocent person and the failure of many States to ensure that innocent persons are not sentenced to death, a Federal statute assuring the availability of DNA testing and a chance to present the results of testing in court is a congruent and proportional prophylactic measure to prevent constitutional injuries from occurring.[17]

---

15 *See* Section 101, Innocence Protection Act, *supra* note 11.

16 *See* Section 102, Innocence Protection Act, *supra* note 11.

17 *Id.*

It should be stressed that, as far back as 1993, a U.S. federal court held, by a majority, that "a persuasive showing of innocence made after trial would render the execution of an inmate unconstitutional."[18] Clearly, the qualification "shocking the conscience and offending standards of decency," as well as "constitutional harm," touch upon obligations *erga omnes*.

C. STATE RESPONSIBILITIES *VIS-À-VIS* THE PROTECTION AGAINST MISCARRIAGE OF JUSTICE: THE ILC ARTICLES ON STATE RESPONSIBILITY

The second reason justifying the qualification of the protection against miscarriages of justice as an obligation *erga omnes* arises from the argument that such protection also involves state responsibilities, inasmuch as governments in their criminal law systems incorporate adequate supervisory systems, as well as mechanisms to reduce the risk of wrongful convictions.

Any state that is not able or willing to burden its criminal justice system with such responsibility is not seriously engaged in designing criminal justice systems that are capable of protecting the innocent. As Senator Leahy remarked in his introduction of the Innocence Protection Act of 2001: "Good prosecutors want to convict the right person, not to get a conviction that may be a mistake, and . . . leave the real culprit in the clear."[19]

State responsibility to protect the innocent and to reduce and redress wrongful convictions may derive from the fundamental human right of every person to freedom of liberty enshrined by Article 5 of the European Convention on Human Rights (ECHR) and Article 9 of the International Covenant on Civil and Political Rights (ICCPR).[20] This right is to be guaranteed by states in relation to its citizens and, due to its direct effect within national criminal jurisdictions, invocable by detainees who challenge the legitimacy of their convictions. In addition, preventing and

---

18 *See* Herrera v. Collins, 506 U.S. 390 (1993).

19 *See* Senator Patrick Leahy's remarks on the introduction of the Innocence Protection Act of 2001, S. 486, 107th Cong. (2001). *See also* Patrick Leahy, *The Innocence Protection Act of 2001*, 29 HOFSTRA L. REV. 1113–54 (2001).

20 For the issue of state responsibility *see also* Chapter 12.

redressing miscarriages of justice is of interest to the international legal community as such, and is not merely restricted to the parties to the criminal proceedings. Again, U.S. Senator Leahy's observations merit attention: "By passing it [the Innocence Protection Act of 2001] we can send a message about the values of fundamental justice that unite all Americans, and by passing it, we can substantially reduce the risk of executing innocent people. We have had a constructive debate, and we have made a noble commitment. It is now time to act."[21] His concluding remarks—that "it is a time for fulfilling the commitments we have made to the American people. And it is a time for action"—reinforce the need for an analysis of the procedures and practices called for in this field within both international and national criminal law.

Based on the foregoing, it is therefore arguable that failure on the part of states to protect against miscarriages of justice falls within the ambit of Articles 1 and 2 of the Articles on the Responsibility of States for Internationally Wrongful Acts adopted by the International Law Commission (ILC) on August 9, 2001. Article 1 of this ILC instrument promulgates the fundamental principle that a breach of international law by a state entails its international responsibility. An internationally wrongful act of a state may consist of one or more actions or omissions or a combination of both.[22] These international wrongful acts include violations of fundamental human rights. As can be derived from the *Barcelona Traction* case, every state, by virtue of its membership in the international community, has a legal interest in the protection of certain basic rights and the fulfilment of certain essential obligations, in which connection the Court mentions the principles and rules concerning the basic rights of the human person.[23] The ILC Articles on State Responsibility, which set forth the constituent elements required to establish the existence of an internationally wrongful act of a state, underscore state responsibility to protect against miscarriages of justice in Article 2:

(1) First, the action or mission must be attributable to the state under international law;

---

21 Leahy, *supra* note 19, at 1117.

22 *See* James Crawford, The International Law Commission's Articles on State Responsibility 77 (2002).

23 *See Barcelona Traction* case, *supra* note 3, at 79.

(2) Second, such (non)action must constitute a breach of an international legal obligation of the state.

As to the element under (1), recourse can be had to:

(1) The ICJ's judgment in the *Diplomatic and Consular Staff* case, in which the court held that the responsibility of Iran consisted of the "inaction" of its authorities who "failed to take appropriate steps" in circumstances where steps were clearly called for;[24]

(2) The judgment of the Inter-American Commission on Human Rights in the *Velasquez Rodriguez* case, in which the Court held that under international law "a state is responsible for the acts of its agents undertaken in their official capacity and for their omissions;"[25] or

(3) The judgment of May 18, 1999, in the English Supreme Court of Judicature Queen's Bench Divisional Court in *Criminal Cases Review Commission* ex parte *Maria Pearson*. This case dealt with an application of Maria Pearson to the Court of Appeal challenging the decision of the Criminal Cases Review Commission not to refer her conviction of murder (sentence of life imprisonment) to the Court of Appeal Criminal Division.[26] It is important to note that in paragraph 7 the Lord Chief Justice holds that "it is essential to the health and proper functioning of a modern democracy that the citizen accused of crime should be fairly tried and adequately protected against the risk and consequences of wrongful conviction."

The British *Pearson* case, which will be discussed in more detail in Chapter 7, thus specifically refers to the protection against wrongful convictions as being part of a "modern democracy."

---

24 *See* U.S. Diplomatic and Consular Staff in Teheran, Judgment 1980 I.C.J. 31–32, paras. 63 and 67.

25 *See* Velasquez Rodriguez case, Inter-Am. Commission on Human Rights (1989), para. 170.

26 *See* R. v. Criminal Cases Review Commission *ex parte* Pearson, CRIM. L. REV. 732–34 (1999), ALL ER 498 (1999).

Based on these three precedents, albeit rendered in different contexts, it is tenable that omissions on the part of government officials, in that they negligently fail to protect against miscarriages of justice, fulfill the two elements of Article 2 of the ILC's Articles on the Responsibility of States for Internationally Wrongful Acts, and thus establish state responsibility. As a result, these observations underscore the relevance of obligations *erga omnes* to protection against, and redressing of, miscarriages of justice.

CHAPTER 3

CAUSES AND PRE-DISPOSING FACTORS OF MISCARRIAGES OF JUSTICE: A LEGAL OVERVIEW

A. CLEAR AND PRESENT DANGERS

Analyzing the phenomenon of miscarriages of justice in criminal cases, two different elements should be distinguished: the causes of miscarriages of justice within criminal cases, and the pre-disposing factors that may fuel miscarriages of justice.

With respect to the causes, attention can be drawn to the four categories of causes that underlie miscarriages of justice in criminal cases. Quoting from a study by Bedau and Radelet, Gudjonsson describes these as:

> (1) *Errors caused by police investigation prior to trial.* These kinds of error were present in 23% of the sample. The largest source of error was false confession, which was present in 49 (14 percent) cases. This typically involved the police "coercing" a confession out of suspects by subjecting them to rigorous interrogation techniques and tactics. However, there were cases of voluntary confessions. In one case an innocent man confessed to murder in order to "impress" his girlfriend. In another case, a woman confessed and pleaded guilty to a murder she had not committed in an attempt to hide the fact that at the time of the murder she was having sexual intercourse! Other police errors involved negligence and over-zealous police work. There were also cases where the police had secured conviction of an innocent defendant by threatening witnesses who were prepared to testify in his favour.

(2) *Errors caused by the prosecution prior to or during the trial.* This was evident in 50 (14 percent) cases and the most common type of error was the suppression of exculpatory evidence (35 cases).

(3) *Errors caused by prosecution witnesses.* This type of error comprised perjury (117 cases) and mistaken person identification (56 cases).

(4) *Miscellaneous sources of error.* These included misleading circumstantial evidence (9 percent), insufficient consideration of alibi evidence (13 percent), incompetence of defence counsel (3 percent), and public demand and outrage (20 percent). The fact that in 70 cases public outrage and pressure appeared to have seriously influenced the trials' outcome highlights the difficulties involved in trying notorious cases.[1]

As to the issue of pre-disposing factors in this regard, considerable research has been done in the past decade on the pre-disposing factors and causes of miscarriages of justice. This research is mainly due to the increased attention to the subject of wrongful convictions. This attention is fueled by awareness that miscarriages of justice occur, and the reality that indeed miscarriages of justice have increasingly emerged in the last three decades. A reason for this development may be found in the much-publicized 1985 ruling in the U.S. case against Rubin "Hurricane" Carter, [2] who was released after being wrongfully convicted and detained for 19 years.[3] Judge Sarokin opined in his ruling that "there is a substantial danger that our society, concerned about the growth of crime, will retreat from the safeguards and rights accorded to the accused by the Constitution. The need to combat crime should never be utilized to justify an erosion of our fundamental guarantees. Indeed, the growing volume of criminal cases should makes us even more vigilant; the greater the *quantity*, the greater the risk to the *quality* of justice."[4]

---

1 Gisli H. Gudjonsson, The Psychology of Interrogations, Confessions and Testimony 210–11 (1993).

2 In 1999, a movie was made of this case titled *The Hurricane*.

3 *See* for miscarriages in the U.S. system, Chapters 3, 4, and 7.

4 *See* Carter v. Rafferty, 621 F. Supp. 533 (D.N.J. 1985).

Indeed, there is enormous pressure on the police and judicial authorities to resolve a criminal case in which the "perpetrator" is presented to the public, especially in high profile cases such as "the Hurricane." In this regard, research reveals that most miscarriages of justice arise from three common pre-disposing factors:

(1) Police and judicial authorities are confronted with considerable (political) pressure to "resolve" the case in that a perpetrator is presented and a conviction is rendered.[5]

(2) In most cases, governmental (prosecutorial) authorities assume that they have found and are prosecuting the right person. In addition, prosecutions on this assumption often relate to accused persons who are outsiders to the dominant community, a circumstance that reinforces prosecutorial assumptions that the right person is being prosecuted. This phenomenon, sometimes also referred to as a form of "tunnel vision," is exemplified by the Irish Republican Army (IRA) cases mentioned in this book,[6] as well as several high profile miscarriages of justice cases in the United States and Canada. Racial prejudice and ethnicity (e.g., when dealing with an indigenous accused) seem to be potent forces in establishing bias and establishing a fertile ground for wrongful convictions.[7] The Canadian *Milgaard* case is illustrative of this factor. The *Milgaard* case shows that a person who is considered to be an "outsider" by the community is especially vulnerable to wrongful prosecutions and convictions. David Milgaard was a drug-using teenager traveling to Saskatoon with two friends when Gail Miller, a young nursing assistant, was raped and murdered on a cold winter night. The case was high profile; and when another drug-using teenager implicated Milgaard during police questioning about another matter (a common occurrence), police quickly built a case based on the evidence from Milgaard's friends and

---

5 *See* Dianne L. Martin, *The Police Role in Wrongful Convictions: An International Comparative Study, in* WRONGLY CONVICTED: PERSPECTIVES ON FAILED JUSTICE 83 (Saundra D. Westervelt & John A. Humphrey eds., 2001).

6 *See* Chapter 7.

7 *See also* Martin, *supra* note 5, at 85.

on a rambling, drug-induced statement by Milgaard himself. It took 23 years of constant pressure from and reinvestigation by Joyce Milgaard (the accused's mother), the New Jersey-based Centurion Ministries, and others to finally unravel the conviction. Approximately six years after Milgaard's release from prison, DNA testing confirmed his innocence and implicated another man; and in November 1999, a serial rapist named Larry Fisher, who was living just blocks away from the murder scene, was convicted of Gail Miller's murder. It came to light that, although police had known about Fisher and the seven similar rapes and knife attacks he had committed, the *Milgaard* prosecution had ensured that the defense never learned of his existence.[8]

(3) A criminal prosecution may rest on unreliable evidence or evidence susceptible to abuse of process by police or prosecution. Such evidence may include:
- eyewitness evidence;
- evidence obtained from informants;
- confessions; and
- forensic evidence based on hypothetical interpretations.[9]

As will be set out in this book, many cases exist that justify the conclusion that these four types of unreliable evidence are propelled by intuitive forces that are difficult to counter-balance. Often this type of evidence is presented by police and prosecutors as convincing evidence. Yet these types have led to a significant number of wrongful convictions.[10] The problem with these forms of evidence lies not only in their collection, but also in the way they are presented in "dossiers" and at trial. The presentation of such evidence, in that it allegedly qualifies as "persuasive" without revealing any nuances, may give false impressions to judges and juries, inducing them to simply adopt the reasoning of police and prosecution. It is exactly this "circularity of reasoning" that forms a potent factor in wrongful convictions.[11]

---

8 *See* Martin, *supra* note 5, at 86–87.

9 *Id.* at 88.

10 *Id.*

11 *Id.*

Wrongful conviction arises from irregularities and incompetence at every stage of the criminal justice process: investigatory, pre-trial, trial, and appellate. More particularly, the following contributory factors, among others, may be identified: false accusations, misleading police investigative work, inept defense counsel, misperceptions by prosecutors of their role, assumption of an accused's guilt by actors in the criminal justice system, community pressure for a conviction, inadequate identification evidence, perjury, false confessions, inadequate or misinterpreted forensic evidence, judicial bias, poor presentation of an appellate case, and difficulty in having fresh evidence admitted at the appellate stage.[12] In some cases, such as the *Central Park Jogger* case,[13] a combination of these factors in the criminal justice system have prevented the court from functioning effectively and fairly.

The ensuing chapters will deal with three main categories of causes of miscarriages of justice that may occur, and actually have occurred, both in national and international criminal cases. These are: miscarriages of justice originating from disclosure deficiencies (Chapter 4); miscarriages of justice originating from false or unreliable confessions and guilty pleas (Chapter 5); and miscarriages of justice originating from identification evidence (Chapter 6).

---

[12] *See* James McCloskey, *Convicting the Innocent*, 2 CRIMINAL JUSTICE ETHICS 54–59 (1989). Mr. McCloskey is Head of the Centurion Ministries, the organization that investigated the Canadian *David Milgaard* case.

[13] *See* Chapter 7.

CHAPTER 4

MISCARRIAGES OF JUSTICE ORIGINATING FROM DISCLOSURE DEFICIENCIES IN CRIMINAL CASES

A. DISCLOSURE FAILURES AS GROUND FOR RETRIALS: COMMON LAW STANDARDS AND EXAMPLES

This chapter will delve more deeply into one of the most fundamental causes of miscarriages of justice in international criminal cases, namely failure on the part of police and/or prosecution to timely, adequately, and fairly disclose potentially exculpatory evidence to the judge, juries, and defense.

1. Disclosure Requirements Set Forth by the U.S. Supreme Court

Concealment of evidence favorable to the defense is one of the main causes of wrongful convictions.[1] In *Brady v. Maryland* (1963), the U.S. Supreme Court set forth the requirement that police and prosecutors must refrain from continuing a criminal prosecution while they are aware of the existence of exculpatory evidence for the accused, which they are withholding from the judges and defense.

The U.S. Supreme Court has defined the following disclosure obligations on this area:

(1) Disclosure requirements extend to documents and information affecting the reliability or credibility of key prosecution witnesses.[2] In this regard it is said that within the U.S.

---

1 *See* George Castelle & Elizabeth Loftus, *Misinformation and Wrongful Convictions, in* WRONGLY CONVICTED: PERSPECTIVES ON FAILED JUSTICE 26 (Saundra D. Westervelt & John A. Humphrey eds., 2001).

2 *See* Giglio v. United States, 405 U.S. 105 (1972).

system, a reviewing court will not overturn a conviction because the prosecution failed to disclose exculpatory evidence, unless this evidence would have likely led to a different judicial outcome.[3]

(2) The prosecution is under an obligation to ensure that all procedures and regulations are in place to effectively communicate all exculpatory evidence from the police to the prosecution and ultimately to the defense.[4]

The foundation of the disclosure system, according to the U.S. Supreme Court, lies in the notion of a fair trial. In *Brady v. Maryland*, the Court expressly held that "society wins not only when the guilty are convicted but when the trials are fair." There can be no fair trial when the exculpatory disclosure system does not function properly. Only when this is seriously contemplated in law practice can miscarriages of justice be foreseen and prevented.[5]

2. Basic Disclosure Conditions Under U.K. Law

Within common law practice, the failure of disclosure can be grounds for a retrial. U.K. case law shows that, in this respect, a relatively low standard is applied. Two examples merit special attention. In the first place, is the U.K. case of *R. v. Kamara*, which will be discussed further in Chapter 6.[6] This case led to a retrial in May 2000. A summary follows of the events that led to this retrial.

On December 16, 1981, in the Crown Court of Liverpool before Justice McCowan, Mr. Kamara was convicted of murder and robbery. He was sentenced to life imprisonment. He had been jointly indicted with Raymond David Gilbert, who pleaded guilty at a critical point in the trial. On March 24, 1983, the Court of Appeal Criminal Division (CACD) heard and dismissed Kamara's renewed application for leave

---

3 *See* Strickler v. Green, 527 U.S. 263 (1999).

4 *See also* Kyles v. Whitley, 514 U.S. 419 (1995).

5 *See also* Castelle & Loftus, *supra* note 1, at 27.

6 *See* Judgment Court of Appeal, Case No. 9902769X4. Criminal Division on Appeal from Liverpool Crown Court, May 9, 2000.

to appeal against conviction. Kamara had appealed upon a reference by the Criminal Case Review Commission (CCRC) pursuant to Section 9 of the Criminal Appeal Act 1995.[7] Section 13 of this Act provides that a reference should be made if the CCRC considers that there is a real possibility that the conviction would not be upheld were the reference to be made. The CCRC came to the conclusion that there was such a real possibility, arising out of:

(1) the potential unfairness of the identification evidence;[8]

(2) the failure of the police to disclose some 201 witness statements taken during the course of the investigation, which were deemed "non-material" despite the fact that some involved sightings of possible suspects near the scene of the crime; and

(3) the failure to direct the jury as to the special need for caution in relation to the evidence of the remand prisoners.

The second of these grounds related to 201 statements that were taken by the police in the course of the original enquiries and not discovered at the time of the original trial. The CCRC concluded that the non-disclosure was a breach of the Attorney-General's Guidelines of 1976[9] (specifically, Guideline 5), which were in place at the time, thus disadvantaging the defense. The facts underlying this non-disclosure shed light on the retrial options once the issue arose. On July 16, 1981, the solicitors for the co-accused of Kamara, Mr. Gilbert, requested the names and addresses of all persons interviewed during the investigation. On August 13, the Department of the Public Prosecutor (DPP) sent a letter to Kamara's then solicitors and the solicitors for Gilbert setting out the names and addresses of 54 "known material witnesses to [to be] called by the prosecution." Gilbert's solicitors replied asking for copies of the statements. On about August 19, the brief for the prosecution was submitted. Attached to the brief were the 54 statements in a bundle entitled "Statements of witnesses not tendered" and a further bundle (number 16) entitled "Non-material statements" which contained the 201 state-

7 *See* Chapter 6.

8 *Id.*

9 912 Hansard No. 115.

ments. On September 3, the DPP wrote a letter to Gilbert's solicitors offering them arrangements to read the 54 statements. Prosecution counsel looked at bundle 16 and made various annotations. He advised in writing on September 15 that:

> There are a number of witnesses in the non-material witnesses file whose evidence might in some circumstances be viewed as material. In the circumstances, I would normally list those witnesses and advise that a further letter be sent detailing their names and addresses to the Defence. However, one of the requests made by Messrs Canter Levin & Company on behalf of Gilbert in their letter dated the 7th August 1981 is to be given access to all the statements of people interviewed and not called. In the particular circumstances of this case, I can see no good reason why that facility should not be provided both as to those considered by the Crown material and those considered not to be material. Although such access will avoid the need to send a further letter and I [Prosecution counsel] advise that access should therefore be given to the solicitors of Kamara and Gilbert.

The Court of Appeal, judging that Kamara's conviction was unsafe, said "most regrettably, the existence of those 201 statements was never disclosed. [The Crown] accepts that they should have been disclosed. On the material available before us, it appears that the fault for that lies within the office of the DPP."[10]

A second case, which illustrates the relatively low standard for allowing a retrial on the basis of disclosure failures, forms the *Quiddington* case.[11] Mr. Quiddington was initially convicted for arson. However, during his trial the police investigators did not reveal the presence of an exculpatory videotape. Ultimately the Court of Appeal quashed the conviction holding that "the new material which has led to us quashing the conviction will not, or may not be decisive and that the case against the appellant remains a significant one. Whether, in the end, that is the view formed by the jury and whether they are satisfied to the high standard that is required, is precisely why we will have a jury to resolve the issues."

---

10 *Id.* at 11–12.

11 *See* R. v. Criminal Cases Review Commission, *ex* Quiddington, Case No. 200001289/W2, Aug. 3, 2000. especially paras. 45 and 83.

Importantly, despite the discovery of new exculpatory evidence for Mr. Quiddington, the Court of Appeal ascertained that, as such, sufficient evidence was available to uphold the initial conviction. Yet, the Court of Appeal deemed it appropriate to reopen the case and allow a jury to reconsider the case on the basis of both the existing and new evidence. This case may therefore be illustrative for applying an extensive threshold when it concerns the eligibility of criminal cases for review on the basis of disclosure failures.

In conclusion, it can be said that non-compliance with fundamental disclosure obligations on the part of the prosecution, as it undermines the integrity of the criminal process, constitutes a valid retrial ground within common law systems when it renders a conviction unsafe. Such a conclusion is also warranted in civil law systems.[12] The next sections will analyze the criteria for this retrial possibility.

B. THE EXTENT OF DISCLOSURE OBLIGATIONS IN CRIMINAL CASES: *R. V. WARD*

The essential importance of timely disclosure of evidence, which is potentially exculpatory, is illustrated persuasively in the landmark case of *R. v. Ward*.[13] For two reasons, the *Ward* case is especially relevant to miscarriages of justice:

(1) The question whether any failure to disclose to the defense potential exculpatory evidence may qualify as a miscarriage of justice; and

(2) The question whether fresh medical evidence, indicating that prior confessions of a convicted person were untrue, can qualify as a new fact that justifies a revision of a criminal case.

This section will assess Question (1). Question (2) is dealt with in Chapter 5.

---

12 *See* for a landmark case in the Dutch legal system: Schiedammer Homicide case, LJN AS1872, Judgment Dutch Supreme Court, Jan. 25, 2005; *see further* Chapter 7.

13 *See* R. v. Ward, 1 W.L.R. 619, 96 Crim. App. R. 1, 2 ALL ER 577 (1993), Court of Appeal (Criminal Division).

In the *Ward* case, the accused, Judith Theresa Ward, was convicted and sentenced to life imprisonment on 12 counts of murder and to 30 years imprisonment on three charges of causing an explosion likely to endanger life or property. These charges related to both a 1973 bomb explosion in London, injuring about a dozen people and causing extensive damage, and a 1977 bomb explosion on a coach carrying soldiers and their families on the M62 motorway, causing the death of 12 passengers. Furthermore, Ward was convicted for her alleged involvement in another bomb explosion injuring many persons. All of the bombings were believed to have been the work of the Irish Republican Army (IRA). The convictions of Ward rested mainly on:

(1) evidence of confession and admissions she had made to the police; and

(2) expert evidence from government forensic scientists that traces of nitroglycerine (NG) had been found on her person after the last bombing and that similar traces had been found in a caravan where Ward had been staying after the second bombing (of the coach).

On September 17, 1991, the Home Secretary referred Ward's case to the Court of Appeal pursuant to Section 17(1)(a) of the Criminal Appeal Act 1968.[14] The letter stated that the reason for this referral was:

(1) Concern about the validity of the scientific evidence at the trial. In particular, earlier investigations, which had led to the 1992 appeal in *R. v. McIlkenny et al.*,[15] cast, according to the Court of Appeal, considerable doubt on the validity of the opinions expressed by forensic expert Dr. Frank Scuse, a chemist from the Home Office Forensic Science Laboratory, who acted as prosecution witness in Ward's case, as the conviction in the *McIlkenny et al.* case was based on the use of a test similar to that used in Ward's case.

(2) Scientific investigation conducted in connection with the inquiry by Sir John May into the case of the Maguire fam-

---

14 *See* for this Act, Section C.

15 *See* 93 Crim. App. R. 287, the so-called *Birmingham Six*. For this case, *see* Chapter 7.

> ily, in 1992,[16] showed that other substances may give similar test results as NG and thus raised the possibility that what appeared to be scientific proof of the presence of NG on Ward's hands, on her baggage, and in the caravan may have been due to the presence of some other substance.[17]

During the referral by the Home Secretary and subsequent appeal, counsel for Ward also raised the following independent appeal grounds:

(1) Before and at the trial, there was a material irregularity in the failure of the prosecution to disclose to the defense relevant evidence that the prosecution was obliged to disclose. This non-disclosure related to evidence that was relevant to the case;

(2) Fresh evidence was made available in appeal that cast considerable doubt on the validity of parts of the scientific evidence given on behalf of the Crown at trial; and

(3) Fresh evidence established that, at and before the time of the trial, Miss Ward was suffering from a personality disorder so severe and deep-rooted that none of the admissions that she had made could be relied upon as being true.[18]

These appeal grounds were based on the fact that in Ward's case, the disclosure of scientific evidence was "woefully deficient."[19] Three senior forensic scientists acting for the Crown, according to the Court of Appeal, "took the law into their hands and concealed from the prosecution, the defence and the court, matters which might have changed the course of the trial. The catalogue of lamentable omissions included failures to reveal actual test results, the failure to reveal discrepant RF values, the suppression of . . . experimental data [which was exculpatory], the misrepresentation of the first firing cell test results, the concealment of subsequent positive firing cell tests results, economical witness statements calculated to obstruct enquiry by the oral evidence

---

16 *See* 94 Crim. App. R. 133 whereby the convictions in that case were quashed; *see* Chapter 7.

17 R. v. Ward, *supra* note 13, 96 Crim. App. R., at 18.

18 *Id.*

19 *Id.* at 15.

at the trial in the course of which senior (forensic) scientists knowingly placed a false and distorted scientific picture before the jury." Accordingly, the Court held that "on the scientific case deployed against her, Miss Ward did not have a fair trial."[20]

C. JUDICIAL RELATIONSHIP BETWEEN DISCLOSURE OF EVIDENCE AND MISCARRIAGES OF JUSTICE

In *R. v. Ward*, the Court of Appeal illuminated the causal link between the issue of disclosure of evidence and potential miscarriages of justice. Particularly, it was faced with the questions:

(1) whether non-disclosure at trial of relevant evidence, which should have been disclosed by the prosecution, amounts to a "material irregularity" in the course of the trial; and

(2) whether the convictions of Ward were "unsafe and unsatisfactory" due to the unreliability of her confessions and the scientific evidence adduced against her.

Based upon the 1992 judgment of the Court of Appeal in *R. v. Maguire et al.*, the Appeal judges in *R. v. Ward* reaffirmed that the failure of the prosecution to disclose to the defense evidence that ought to have been disclosed is an "irregularity in the course of the trial" pursuant to Section 2(1)(c) of the Criminal Appeal Act 1968, whereby it acknowledges that the reason for non-disclosure is "irrelevant."[21] According to the Court of Appeal, not every material irregularity implies a miscarriage of justice; yet non-disclosure is a potent source of injustice although, even with the benefit of hindsight, it will often be difficult to say whether or not an undisclosed item of evidence might have shifted the balance or opened up a new line of defense.[22] However, the Court formulates two guidelines:

(1) Failure to disclose may individually, as well as collectively, constitute a material irregularity as meant above;

---

20 *Id.*

21 *Id.* at 22.

22 *Id.*

(2) The Court of Appeal is mindful of the fact that "the last 18 years have brought considerable advances in medical and forensic science."[23] As a consequence, the Court holds that in deciding whether a verdict is "safe and satisfactory" or whether there has been a miscarriage of justice, "we must clearly take account of all of the knowledge and experience which is available to us in 1992."[24] This means that the Court of Appeal pursues an extensive application of the term "miscarriage of justice," the determination of which should be assessed *ex nunc*, namely on the basis of all the knowledge and material that exists at the time of review of the conviction.

In this regard, the approach in *R. v. Ward* could serve as a general guideline for future cases as to how to determine when a conviction is not safe.

D. JUDICIAL AND LEGAL-ETHICAL IMPLICATIONS OF NON-DISCLOSURE OF FORENSIC EVIDENCE FOR MISCARRIAGES OF JUSTICE

The Court of Appeal in *R. v. Ward* was confronted with a "most extraordinary case"[25] in that the role of the prosecution's scientific evidence at trial against Ward was to lend cogent support to the reliability of her confessions.[26] As to this particular supporting forensic evidence, the Court said that "the non-disclosure of evidence by the forensic scientists who gave evidence for the prosecution is a matter whose significance must be considered in the context of the scientific evidence as a whole."[27] This observation may be seen as a principle for future cases.

Based on these observations and principles, the Court arrived at the following findings, which are highly relevant for the adjudication of future criminal cases in view of (preventing) miscarriages of justice:

(1) On page 50 of the ruling, the Court of Appeal unravels the legal-ethical rationale of disclosure of forensic evidence to

---

23 *Id.* at 23.

24 *Id.*

25 *Id.* at 66.

26 *Id.* at 42.

27 *Id.*

an accused, asserting that "An incident of a defendant's right to a fair trial is a right to timely disclosure by the prosecution, that is, whether such matters strengthen or weaken the prosecution case or assist the defence case."

(2) Importantly, the court holds that "this duty exists whether or not a specific request for disclosure of details of scientific evidence is made by the defense."[28] The Appeal judges in the *Ward* case reiterate this notion on pages 52–53 of the judgment in more precise words, namely by stressing that the duty of disclosure of scientific evidence exists "irrespective of any request by the defence," and by saying that "it is also not limited to documentation on which the opinion or findings of an expert is based." For the Court of Appeal, this duty extends "to anything which may arguably assist the defence." The Court qualifies it as "a positive duty," which, in the context of scientific evidence, "obliges the prosecution to make full and proper enquiries from forensic scientists in order to ascertain whether there is discoverable material."[29]

(3) Furthermore, the Court opines that "this duty is continuous; it applies not only in the pre-trial period but also throughout the trial."[30]

(4) The Court observes that "the materiality of evidence on the scientific side of a case may sometimes be overlooked before a trial," but "if the significance of the evidence becomes clear during the trial there must be an immediate disclosure to the defence."[31]

In addition, the Court of Appeal in the *Ward* case promulgated some specific ethical norms for forensic scientists acting in criminal cases:

(1) The Court characterizes the relationship between such scientists and police in investigating criminal cases by saying

---

28 *Id.* at 50.

29 *Id.*

30 *Id.*

31 *Id.*

that "the very fact that the police seek their assistance [that of forensic scientists] may create a relationship between the police and the forensic scientists. And the adversarial character of the proceedings tends to promote this process. Forensic scientists employed by the government may come to see their function as helping the police. They may lose their objectivity."[32]

(2) The Court holds that "it is the clear duty of government forensic scientists to assist in a neutral and impartial way in criminal investigations. They must act in the cause of justice."[33] The Court believes that "the surest way of preventing the misuse of scientific evidence is by ensuring that there is a proper understanding of the nature and scope of the prosecution's duty of disclosure."[34]

E. PRACTICAL IMPLICATIONS OF NON-DISCLOSURE OF FORENSIC EVIDENCE FOR MISCARRIAGES OF JUSTICE: THE PRINCIPLE OF EQUALITY OF ARMS

After setting forth the judicial and legal-ethical implications of non-disclosure in the context of miscarriages of justice, which can be read in the *Ward* decision, we now turn to consider several practical implications thereof.

The Court of Appeal ruling inheres an important notion, which goes to the heart of the relationship between miscarriages of justice and disclosure of evidence, i.e., the preservation of the principle of equality of arms. In this regard, the Court holds that "given the undoubted inequality as between prosecution and defense in access to forensic scientists, we [i.e., the Court of Appeal] regard it as of paramount importance that the common law duty of disclosure . . . should be appreciated by those who prosecute and defend in criminal cases."[35] In the light of what has

---

32 *Id.* at 51, in which the Court notes that this is what must have happened in the *Ward* case.

33 *Id.* at 52.

34 *Id.*

35 *Id.* at 53.

been adduced by the Court with respect to the importance of forensic evidence within contemporary international criminal cases, the endorsement of this principle of equality of arms *vis-à-vis* forensic evidence and expert is of perennial concern.

As a practical rule, and in order to advance the principle of equality of arms, the Court sets forth that "an expert witness who has carried out or knows of experiments or tests which tend to cast doubt on the opinion he is expressing is . . . under a clear obligation to bring the records of such experiments and tests to the attention of the solicitor who is instructing him so that it may be disclosed to the other party."[36]

The Court of Appeal addresses a topic that is clearly of practical relevance in this area, namely the question of whether, and if so how far, public interest immunity may supersede the disclosure obligation *vis-à-vis* the defense in criminal cases, particularly regarding documents helpful to the defense. In this respect, the Court of Appeal formulates the rule that, in such an event, the prosecution is obliged to give notice to the defense of the asserted right to withhold the documents so that, if necessary, the Court can be asked to rule on the legitimacy of the prosecution's asserted claim.[37] The *Ward* case, in the words of the judges themselves, "powerfully reinforces the view that it would be wrong to allow the prosecution to withhold material documents without giving any notice of that fact to the defence." In the event, in a wholly exceptional case, that the prosecution is not prepared to have the issue of public interest immunity reviewed by a court, "the result must inevitably be that the prosecution will have to be abandoned."[38]

F. DISCLOSURE OBLIGATION STANDARDS

1. General Guidelines

The case of *R. v. Ward* was, as the Court of Appeal itself noted, "a most extraordinary case." It shows that it is essential that those who are responsible for a prosecution, and for the provision of evidence upon

---

36 *Id.* at 55.
37 *Id.* at 56–57.
38 *Id.* at 57.

which the prosecution is based (among them forensic scientists), "should comply with their basic duty to seek to ensure a trial which is fair both to the prosecution . . . and to the accused."[39] Failure to carry out this basic duty, as happened in the *Ward* case, may result in "a grave miscarriage of justice."[40] The importance of the *Ward* judgment is that it promulgates disclosure obligations as not only a legal norm but as a legal-ethical norm to be maintained by police, prosecution, and forensic scientists themselves.

2. Attribution of Non-Disclosure by Police and Scientists to the Crown

Seen from the perspective of these conclusions of the Court of Appeal in *R. v. Ward*, it is not surprising that the appeal judges allowed the appeal and quashed the convictions of Ward on all counts, saying that "in the failure to disclose evidence, some in the possession of the police, some in the possession of the scientists and some in possession of the DPP, there were material irregularities at the trial; and that, having regard to that non-disclosure added to the fresh evidence we have heard, the convictions were all unsafe and unsatisfactory."[41] Notably, according to the Court of Appeal the non-disclosure by both the police and forensic scientists acting on behalf of the Crown can legally be attributed to the Crown itself and thus fall within the legal responsibility of the Crown. Apparently, it is not a prerequisite that the accused proves in this regard bad faith, as such, on the part of these organs; on this issue, the view in *R. v. Ward* differs from the standpoint of the Dutch Supreme Court.[42]

3. "Reasonable Probability Test" as Ground for Retrial

With respect to a uniform retrial standard based on non-compliance with the above-mentioned disclosure obligations, the test as promulgated by the U.S. Supreme Court seems preferable. In *United States v.*

---

39 *Id.* at 67.

40 *Id.*; in the *Ward* case , the Court of Appeal arrives at the overall conclusion that such a "grave" miscarriage of justice occurred.

41 *Id.*

42 *See supra* note 12.

Bagley[43] the Supreme Court came to a certain "materiality" test, which can also be applied within the context of retrial proceedings. According to the judges of the U.S. Supreme Court, "Nondisclosed evidence (. . .) is material only if there is a reasonable probability that, had the evidence been disclosed to the defense, the result of the proceeding would have been different. A 'reasonable probability' is a probability sufficient to undermine confidence in the outcome. This standard is sufficiently flexible to cover cases of prosecutorial failure to disclose evidence favorable to the defense regardless of whether the defense makes no request, a general request, or a specific request."[44]

In the concluding chapter of this book, I will consider this test in the context of an overall and uniform review provision for both civil law and common law jurisdictions.

G. DISCLOSURE OBLIGATIONS UNDER ECHR CASE LAW RELEVANT TO PROTECTION AGAINST MISCARRIAGES OF JUSTICE

1. Competing Interests: Protection of Society Versus Protection of Individuals

As set forth in the previous sections, the extent of disclosure obligations on the part of the prosecution before an international or national criminal court will ultimately rely on moral, social, and political considerations. After all, disclosure obligations within international and domestic criminal tribunals are closely connected to the aim and purposes of such trials, the goals of which, in their turn, are influenced by the same considerations. When one perceives international and national criminal law principally as an instrument to protect society against international criminality, the scope of disclosure obligation will be different compared to the perception of international criminal law as primarily an instrument to protect the rights of individuals against abusive behavior of governments in investigating and prosecuting crimes. Governments will need to assess the different legal policies of criminal law systems themselves. Yet, if criminal trials are see as instrumental to the advance-

43 United States v. Bagley, 473 U.S. 667 (1985).

44 *Id.*

ment of the relevant societal goals, the need arises for some degree of equity in the administration of overarching legal principles. This is particularly true of those principles that are instrumental and decisive in redressing miscarriages of justice.

Since, as we have seen, disclosure of evidence on the part of the government and prosecution is at the heart of the issue of preventing wrongful convictions, the relevant case law of the European Court of Human Rights (ECHR), an international supervisory judicial institution, merits thought. The value of this case law is reinforced in light of its repeated adoption by international and internationalized criminal tribunals.[45]

2. ECHR Disclosure Criteria and Their Transposition onto Retrial Proceedings in Criminal Cases

Disclosure obligations on the part of the prosecution have been perceived by the ECHR as derivative from Article 6 of the European Convention on Human Rights, which article states the right to a fair trial. The ECHR has developed several disclosure criteria that are pertinent for the protection against miscarriages of justice. A summary of these criteria follows.

The prosecution is, in principle, obligated to disclose to the defense "all material evidence in their possession for and against the accused."[46] It is tenable that this principle also extends to a situation in which criminal proceedings have been closed and a convicted person petitions for a retrial, presupposing that such a person has a reasonable interest in disclosure of certain materials that were not disclosed during the initial trial proceedings.[47] In a ruling of December 5, 2005, in *Prosecutor v. Ina Post*,[48] the District Court at the Hague (the Netherlands) held that the applicant bears the burden to establish "a reasonable interest" as to

---

45 *See*, for this topic, GEERT-JAN ALEXANDER KNOOPS, THEORY AND PRACTICE OF INTERNATIONAL AND INTERNATIONALIZED CRIMINAL PROCEEDINGS 15–89 (2005).

46 *See* Dowsett v. U.K., Judgment ECHR June 24, 2003; Judgment ECHR, Edwards and Lewis v. U.K. July 22, 2003,; for this topic in detail *see* KNOOPS, *supra* note 45, at 159–73.

47 *See* Prosecutor v. Ina Post, Judgment District Court of the Hague (Netherlands), Case No. KG 05/1346, Dec. 5, 2005.

48 *Id.*

the disclosure of police records and other materials, such as forensic evidence, which were not revealed during the initial criminal proceedings in that case. In this interim injunction ruling, the Dutch Court was satisfied that the plaintiff, Ms. Post, met this burden. The Court subsequently ordered the Dutch government to release to the defense all forensic evidence in its possession as of 1986 (the year that the criminal case against Ina Post started), in order to allow the defense to conduct forensic investigations in view of a retrial.

The disclosure obligation may also extend to materials that are officially not part of the particular criminal file, but remain in the possession of the government or prosecution, and disclosure of which could be instrumental for the defense case. This motion was set forth in the decision of the European Commission on Human Rights in the *Dev Sol* case.[49] In the *Dev Sol* case the defendant had been denied access to particular documents (photograph albums) because of the investigative interests at stake. Such access was, however, provided to defense counsel. The latter refused to make use of that opportunity on the ground that her client was refused access. After the Supreme Court decided the case, defense counsel filed a complaint on that issue to the European Commission. The Commission subsequently held that it was not contrary to the Convention to deny the defendant (but not his counsel) access to certain documents, given that the photograph albums were required by the prosecution authorities for use in ongoing investigations. In addition, the photograph albums could not be regarded as a decisive element in the defendant's conviction, and therefore the complaint was declared inadmissible by the European Commission.

This decision of the European Commission was preceded by the judgment in the *Dev Sol* case of the Dutch Supreme Court of May 7, 1996,[50] in which the Court acknowledged that, in a criminal case, there may be documents that do not belong to those of the case record (thus not representing "documents of the case record") but that are nevertheless potentially relevant in light of assessing the reliability and trustworthiness of the evidence adduced by the prosecutor. In the *Dev Sol* case, the Dutch Supreme Court held that the defendant, *in principle*,

[49] *See* Decision European Commission on Human Rights, Sept. 9, 1998.

[50] *See* NJ (Dutch Jurisprudence) 1996, No. 687.

should be given access to these documents not belonging to the case record—in principle, because the investigative interest at stake may justify withholding these documents from the defendant.

This approach, based upon the "reasonable interest" criterion, may thus be used by the defense in retrial proceedings, in particular when attempting to redress a putative miscarriage of justice—for instance, for the acquisition of forensic records and documents or even police notes that were not officially part of the case file. It should be borne in mind, however, that, according to the case law of the ECHR, the mere fact that the government or prosecution has (had) access to more materials than those submitted in the case file does not by itself infringe upon the principle of equality of arms. The decisive issue is whether or not the suppressed materials and evidence for or against the accused (convicted person) appear to be of reasonable interest for a retrial.

CHAPTER 5

MISCARRIAGES OF JUSTICE ORIGINATING FROM FALSE OR UNRELIABLE CONFESSIONS AND PLEA AGREEMENTS

A. INTRODUCTION

Closely connected to the phenomenon of miscarriage of justice is the issue of false or unreliable confessions. Several domestic criminal cases in the United States, the Netherlands, and the United Kingdom reveal the relationship between such confessions and miscarriages of justice, in that convictions were overturned by virtue of the establishment of false confessions that underlied the initial conviction.[1] This chapter will assess the implications of this relationship and will do so on the basis of important case law.

B. THE ROLE OF FALSE CONFESSIONS IN INTERNATIONAL CRIMINAL CASES

Although false confessions do occur, their frequency is difficult to estimate. Within international criminal cases, the effects of false confessions are considerable. Not only may such confessions lead to a conviction, but also the psychological consequences after having falsely confessed are grave. The Dutch criminal case of *Prosecutor v. Ina Post* is illustrative of this. In 1987, Post was convicted by a Dutch Court of Appeal for manslaughter and sentenced to six years imprisonment solely on the basis of her own confession, which turned out to be false. Since then, according to psychiatric evaluation, she has never recovered her mental health. In 2003 and 2006, Post petitioned for a

[1] For case law, *see* Chapter 7.

retrial, relying on various expert witness reports that showed the false nature of her confession.[2]

The subject of false confession can be divided into three categories:

(1) Voluntary false confessions. Confessions are made without external pressure by police or third persons; e.g., to protect the real perpetrator.

(2) Coerced-compliant false confessions. These mainly result from improper police interrogation methods.

(3) Coerced-internalized false confessions. Confessions of individuals innocent of the particular crime who, in the course of the investigation, start to believe that they have committed the crime without initially having a concrete recollection of the crime. Gradually, the innocent accused does not trust his or her own memory any more and begins to rely on external information and suggestion, a phenomenon sometimes referred to as the "memory distrust syndrome."[3]

In addition to these situational elements, two subjective factors are determinative for the establishment of false confessions:

(1) The element of "suggestibility," meaning the tendency of the individual to respond in a particular way to suggestions. This mechanism involves the susceptibility of individuals to incorporate information received from other persons into their own memory. For instance, the police suggest to an accused that he or she was seen at the crime scene. Even if this is not true, the accused may state to the Court that he or she "remembers" being there.

(2) The element of "compliance," meaning the tendency of persons to comply with authoritative behavior, which may result

---

2 *See* Dutch Supreme Court Judgment, Feb. 17, 2004, Dutch Jurisprudence (NJ) 2004, 333.

3 *See* S.M. Kassin & K.L. Kiechel, *The Social Psychology of False Confessions: Compliance, Internalization and Confabulation*, 7 PSYCHOL. SCI. 125–28 (1996); S.M. Kassin, *On the Psychology of Confessions: Does Innocence Put Innocents at Risk?*, 2 AM. PSYCHOL. 215–28 (2005).

> in a false confession in order to comply with demands from police authorities. Most accused are sensitive to police authority, and to avoid conflicts during interrogations declare what is beneficial to the police investigation.

Research shows that both suggestibility and compliance constitute risk factors for the occurrence of false confessions.[4] Within the Dutch legal system, a miscarriage of justice occurred when four accused in the *Puttense Homicide* case were led into false confessions, whereby the factor of "suggestibility" was determinative for this. During the retrial proceedings before the Court of Appeal it turned out that the accused were told that their DNA was found on the crime scene, while this was not true. The Appellate Court, after retrial, acquitted the two accused who were each initially sentenced to 12 years' imprisonment.[5]

It is therefore advisable that, prior to police interrogations, the accused should be tested on these two elements in order to verify the vulnerability of the accused to these influences and to forestall the likelihood of a false confession.[6] The same counts for the element of mental retardation.[7]

C. RETRIAL GROUNDS RELATIVE TO FALSE CONFESSIONS IN CRIMINAL CASES

1. False Confessions: Basis for Retrial?

a. False Confessions Revealed by DNA Evidence

An important problem revealed by wrongful convictions, based upon confessions of the accused, is that judges are inclined to attach weight to confessions made to the police and prosecution, even if these con-

---

4 *See* GISLI H. GUDJONSSON, THE PSYCHOLOGY OF INTERROGATIONS AND CONFESSIONS: A HANDBOOK (2003).

5 *See* for this case judgment Dutch Supreme Court, NJ 2001, 564, June 26, 2001, reopening this criminal case on the basis of new forensic evidence; see for the judgment acquitting the accused, Decision Apr. 24, 2002, Court of Appeal Leeuwarden Case Nos. 24-000688-01 and 24-000687-01.

6 *See* Robert Horselenberg & Ton Smeets, *False Confessions*, 14 ADVOCATENBLAD (Journal for the Dutch Bar Association) 623 (2005).

7 *See* Section C and Chapter 12.

fessions are withdrawn.[8] In English and American law, considerable evidentiary weight is attached to a confession that is given freely and voluntarily. Within these legal systems, as a matter of principle, confessions deemed to be involuntary are excluded from evidence.[9] According to these legal systems, confession evidence can be excluded due to police misconduct or because of high suggestibility of the accused, if proven. Compared to American courts, English courts are seemingly pursuing a more restrictive course as to the admissibility of expert witness testimony with respect to the assessment of the validity of confessions.[10]

The relativity of confessions in international criminal cases and their potential for miscarriage of justice was aptly illustrated by the U.S. case against Jerry Frank Townsend. Mr. Townsend (49) was a retarded man who spend 22 years behind bars for six murders he did not commit, notwithstanding his confessions to the police. The police took Townsend to murder scenes and recorded his confessions. In 1980, Townsend was convicted of first-degree murder for the 1973 killings of Naomi Gamble and Barbara Brown in Broward County, Florida. Not only did he confess to these murders, but he also confessed to the murder of 13-year old Sonja Marion in 1979. Eventually, Townsend was cleared by DNA evidence following actions in 1998, when Sonja Marion's mother instructed a police detective to review the Townsend cases. In 2000, DNA testing of a semen sample on the child's shorts implicated another man. Subsequently, further DNA evidence cleared Townsend of two of the six murders. The evidence pointed to another person, and, accordingly, substantial doubt was raised on the accuracy of all the confessions of Townsend. In April 2001, Townsend was also cleared of the two Broward killings on the bases of new DNA testing, eliminating two of his seven life sentences. Ultimately, Townsend was fully discharged and released on June 15, 2001, at the age of 49 after spending 22 years in prison.[11]

The *Townsend* case is also indicative of the importance of verifing the authenticity of a confession on the basis of supporting evidence, such as DNA analysis.

---

8 *See also* Saul M. Kassin & Gisli H. Gudjonsson, *The Psychology of Confession: A Review of the Literature and Issues*, 2 PSYCHOL. SCI. 56 (2004).

9 *See* GISLI H. GUDJONSSON, THE PSYCHOLOGY OF INTERROGATIONS, CONFESSIONS AND TESTIMONY 296 (1993).

10 *Id.* at 297.

11 *Id.*

b. False Confessions and Mental Retardation

In the context of false confessions, the element of mental retardation deserves specific attention when assessing retrial possibilities. Various cases in the United States, as well as in Europe, have proven that mentally retarded individuals are particularly vulnerable to being wrongfully convicted.[12] In light of the observation that most law enforcement officials are not specifically trained to interrogate mentally retarded suspects, the risks of giving false confessions are considerable.

The first example of this increasing risk to miscarriages of justice, was already exemplified by the mentioned case against Jerry Frank Townsend. The confessions of Townsend were largely the consequence of him intending to please authority figures, a common adaptive practice by someone with his mental capacities.[13] The U.S. judge, Scott J. Silverman, of the Miami-Dade Circuit Court expressed that Mr. Townsend was the victim of "an enormous tragedy." After being charged in 1979, Townsend was convicted of two murders and pleaded guilty to four others and a rape. He was serving seven life sentences. Importantly, the IQ of Mr. Townsend was 50–60.[14]

The second example relates to the prosecution of David Vasquez convicted in 1985 for the murder of a woman, after she had been sexually assaulted. It turned out that Vasquez was borderline mentally retarded and confessed to the crime, allegedly submitting details of the crime that were not public. He also could not provide an alibi and was placed near the crime scene by two eyewitnesses. Finally, investigators discovered pubic hairs that resembled those of Vasquez. Vasquez was qualified in Court as having "borderline retarded/low normal" intelligence and was so afraid of being executed that he confessed. Due to this confession, David Vasquez spent five years in prison before he was exonerated. This exoneration derived from DNA testing on evidence collected from other crimes where the real perpetrator used the same methods performed in the murder for which Vasquez was convicted. Vasquez was released in 1989.[15]

---

12 *See* Web site of the American Civil Liberties Union (ACLU), *at* http://www.aclu.org/capital/mentalretardation/10435pub20031209.html (last visited Mar. 15, 2006).

13 *See id.*

14 *See Retarded Man Freed on DNA Evidence* N.Y. TIMES, June 16, 2001.

15 See ACLU Web site, *supra* note 12.

The third case is the prosecution of Earl Washington, which started in 1983. Like Townsend, Washington was an accused who suffered from borderline mental retardation with an IQ of 69, and he was led into a confession for rape and murder of a woman, by police investigators not familiar with interrogating mentally retarded individuals. In 2000, subsequent DNA evidence exonerated Washington for this rape.[16]

These three examples are only a few of many cases that show that mental retardation on the part of the accused has the potential to culminate in miscarriages of justice, when the interrogations of such individuals are not conducted by qualified investigators.

The next sections will specifically go into the prevention of false confessions, in particular the extent to which psychological or psychiatric evidence is admissible to assist a court of law in the determination of the authenticity of confessions, in particular with respect to whether the question of a retrial is justifiable on the basis of a false confession.

2. The Importance of Disclosure of Forensic Evidence for the Determination of False Confessions: *R. v. Ward*

As observed in Chapter 4, the phenomenon of false confession may, to a decisive extent, rely on defects in the prosecution's disclosure obligation of potential exculpatory (forensic) evidence to the defense. The case of *R. v. Ward*, retried by the Court of Appeal (Criminal Division) in the United Kingdom,[17] is illustrative of this topic. It sets forth the following guidelines, which may illuminate the ways in which false confessions cause a miscarriage of justice.

The Court delineates an important basic tenet, namely that "it is rare, but not unknown, for a person who is not subjected to any improper pressure or an inducement to confess to crimes he or she has not committed. It is even more rare for somebody, in such circumstances, to confess to crimes as grave as those for which Miss Ward stood trial. Nevertheless our criminal courts, and all those who owe a duty to do what is neces-

---

16 *See id.*

17 *See* 1 W.L.R. 619, 96 Crim. App. R. 1, 2 ALL ER 577 (1993), Court of Appeal (Criminal Division).

sary to ensure that the courts arrive at proper verdicts, must take account of the possibility that confessions, though not the result of any impropriety, may be untrue."[18] It seems that, with this notion, the Court advocates judicial scrutiny as to the reliance on confessions in capital criminal cases, especially when the confession lies at the heart of the prosecution case.

The Court of Appeal formulates three conditions that should be met in a criminal trial when the prosecution seeks to rely upon a confession or admission, or a series of confessions or admissions, made by the accused person. These conditions must be proven by the prosecution:

(1) The accused spoke or wrote the words alleged;

(2) The confession was made voluntarily, not as result of the use of force or a threat or the holding out of an inducement; and

(3) The confession or admission was true.[19]

With respect to condition (1) the court notes that the tape recording of the great majority of interviews of suspects by the police has resulted in a lessening of allegations that the defendant did not say what he was alleged to have said.[20] The Court is mindful that, even with tape recording, such a dispute can arise in the event it is alleged that a verbal confession was made before arrival at the police station.[21] With respect to condition (2), the Court opines that cases in which it is accepted that a confession was made voluntarily, but nevertheless it is asserted that the confession is wholly untrue, "are rare in the extreme."[22] Yet, despite this apparent rarity, the Court notes that there is "but little authority" on this issue. Therefore, proper disclosure of all the interviews with the accused is of importance.[23] Moreover, existing medical reports, which could shed light on the truthfulness of the accused, fall within the same disclosure

---

18 *Id.*, 96 Crim. App. R., at 67.

19 *Id.* at 57.

20 *Id.*

21 *Id.*

22 *Id.* at 58.

23 *Id.* The Court of Appeal in the *Ward* case concluded that this was clearly not done, several statements of Ward were not disclosed before the trial, statements that were of significance in relation to Ward's reliability.

obligation, as such reports, can serve as control mechanisms for the reliability of the accused's statements.[24]

3. The Admissibility of Evidence of Psychiatrists and Psychologists as to an Accused's Reliability

In *R. v. Ward*, the Court of Appeal in the review of this case was also faced with fresh evidence, principally medical evidence, which could impact upon the reliability of the accused and her confessions. In *R. v. Ward*, this fresh medical evidence before the Court of Appeal concerned the expert testimony of two experts (a psychiatrist and a psychologist) called on behalf of the defense and one psychiatrist called on behalf of the prosecution. The defense experts, in the retrial, held that Ward suffered from a personality disorder long before her arrest in 1974, which mental disorder had a profound effect on her capacity to give a reliable account of herself and her memories to anybody.[25] In particular, the defense expert Gisli Gudjonsson (specialized in research on measuring suggestibility and confabulation) opined, as to the suggestibility of the accused, that she "was abnormally yielding to the misleading questions" and that she had "an abnormal tendency to accept the suggestions offered, which tendency to confabulate fell well outside the normal range."[26] Importantly, the Court of Appeal, relying on other precedents, found this new medical evidence admissible in support of the appeal grounds of defense in *R. v. Ward*, and formulated the following five criteria for such admissibility in a revision case:

(1) The Court delineates the requisite nature of the disorder that must be met, saying that "we conclude on the authorities as they now stand that the expert evidence of a psychiatrist or psychologist may properly be admitted if it is to the effect that a defendant is suffering from a condition not properly described as mental illness, but form a personality disorder so severe as properly to be categorized as mental disorder."[27]

---

[24] *Id.* In this regard the *Ward* case showed that these reports also were insufficiently disclosed to the defense.

[25] *Id.* at 61.

[26] *Id.*

[27] *Id.* at 66.

Thus, what counts is the establishment of a mental disorder and not necessarily a mental illness.

(2) The Court declares that such medical evidence in a revision procedure is only admissible on the issue of whether what a defendant has said in a confession or admission was reliable and therefore likely to have been true.[28] Herewith, a clear link between such evidence and the issue of reliability is established.

(3) The appeal judges stress that this approach is "not to be construed as an open invitation to every defendant who repents of having confessed and seeks to challenge the truth of his confession to seek the aid of a psychiatrist."[29]

(4) The Court holds that where evidence of the "quality and force" of that which was rendered as new medical evidence in Ward's case, the third criterion does not apply and is thus admissible.[30] Thus, on a case-by-case basis, the "quality and force" of newly introduced medical evidence that goes to the reliability of confessions should be assessed by the reviewing court.

(5) As to the question of which criteria should be met in order to overturn a conviction based on confessions of an accused, the decisive questions for the Court of Appeal in *R. v. Ward* ask whether the full availability of medical evidence would have weakened the prosecution's case, strengthened the defense case in seeking to establish Ward's unreliability, or attenuated the strength of forensic evidence as to support or challenge the truth of the confessions.[31]

In this regard the key question seems to be whether the accused, facing criminal charges, has an absolute and enforceable right to have access to an expert witness in order to determine whether a false confession has been made. In a judgment of February 7, 2006, the Dutch Supreme

---

28 *Id.*

29 *Id.*

30 *Id.*

31 *Id.* at 67.

Court came to a negative answer to this question, saying that such a view did not find support in the law and that a denial of the accused's request to have his false confession examined by a forensic psychologist does not amount to a violation of Article 6 of the European Convention of Human Rights.[32]

D. INVOLUNTARY STATEMENTS WITHIN INTERNATIONAL CRIMINAL PROCEEDINGS: RETRIAL CONSEQUENCES

As has been shown in the preceding sections, miscarriages of justice may arise from unreliable confessions in criminal cases. The question now merits attention to whether statements of defendants as such, without being tantamount to a confession, can lead to wrongful convictions in criminal cases. In this regard, the practice of the International Criminal Tribunal for the Former Yugoslavia (ICTY) may be instructive, as ICTY case law offers guidelines on scrutinizing the voluntariness of statements given by accused to investigators and/or the prosecution, and also on the proper procedure to be followed in obtaining such statements. These two elements—voluntariness of accused's statements, and procedure in obtaining such statements—will be dealt with in this section, based on ICTY case law, which may be extrapolated to national criminal cases.

1. Judicial Supervision on Involuntariness of Accused's Statements

In general, it can be said that the practice of international criminal courts up till now, with respect to the admission of statements of accused and confessions into evidence (against the accused), has been to allow such admission unless the latter is able to establish that these statements should be excluded due to their involuntary nature. The burden of proof for this involuntariness rests on the accused (Rule 92 of the Rules of Procedure in Evidence (RPE) of the ICTY and the International Criminal Tribunal for Rwanda (ICTR)).[33]

---

32 See Judgment Dutch Supreme Court, NJ 2006, 139, Feb. 7, 2006.

33 *See* RICHARD MAY & MARIEKE WIERDA, INTERNATIONAL CRIMINAL EVIDENCE 292 (2002).

The rules of these international tribunals, in order to prevent miscarriages of justice due to involuntary statements, have developed a set of principles tantamount to mandatory obligations for the prosecution when it intends to take down statements of accused persons. The two main principles are:

(1) Counsel shall be present during the interview;[34] and

(2) The questioning is audio or video recorded.[35]

In particular, two decisions of the ICTY have set forth important parameters as to how to determine the involuntariness of statements of the accused.

In the first case, *Prosecutor v. Halilovic*, the ICTY Appeals Chamber judges were faced with an argument of the accused saying that the record of his interview was inadmissible due to the alleged conduct of the prosecution in persuading the accused to agree to give the interview. In granting the appeal of the accused, the Appeals Chamber formulated the following guidelines.[36]

In paragraph 14 it is held that:

> the Rules do not permit a record of an interview with the accused to be tendered into evidence unless the accused has chosen to testify or has consented to the tender . . . the Appeals Chamber does not agree that the Rules impose such a categorical restriction. The Rules instead grant Trial Chambers considerable discretion on evidentiary matters; in particular Rule 89(C) states that a "Chamber may admit any relevant evidence which it deems to have probative value." Here the Trial Chamber was satisfied that the record of interview was relevant and probative, and the Appellant does not dispute these points. The Trial Chamber therefore had the discretion to admit the record, at least so long as doing so did not violate any of the specific restrictions outlined

---

34 *See* ICTY and ICTR Rule 63.

35 *Id.*

36 *See* Prosecutor v. Halilovic, Decision on Interlocutory Appeal Concerning Admission of Record of Interview of the Accused from the bar Table, Case No. IT-01-48, Aug. 19, 2005.

> in the remainder of the Rules, nor the general principle of Rule 89(B) requiring application of " rules of evidence which will best favour a fair determination of the matter before it and are consonant with the spirit of the Statute and the general principles of law."

As for the interference with the right against self-incrimination, the Appeals Chamber opined that:

> the Appeals Chamber does not find that fairness or the "spirit of the Statute and general principles of law" require that the admissibility of an accused's prior statements turn on whether he has agreed to testify or consented to the admission. The Appellant's argument to the contrary rests implicitly on the right of an accused against self-incrimination. An accused has the right to refuse to give statements incriminating himself prior to trial, and he had the right to refuse to testify at trial. But where the accused has freely and voluntarily made statements prior to trial, he cannot later on choose to invoke his right against self-incrimination retroactively to shield those statements from being introduced, provided he was informed about his right to remain silent before giving this statement; there is, however, a presumption that he knows about this right if he is assisted by counsel. Nor does the Appellant point to any provision of the Rules or rules of customary international law that specifically imposes such a restriction on the admission of an accused's prior statements. The Appeals Chamber therefore concludes that no such rules exists.[37]

It is important to assess the question whether and when inducement of the accused by the prosecution, in the course of obtaining statements, may occur and whether this impacts on the admissibility of statements. To this end, the ICTY Appeals Chamber develops the following thoughts in paragraphs 35–39 of *Halilovic:*

> The Appeals Chamber does not agree that the Prosecution's inability to grant the Appellant provisional release means that the Prosecution's statement that full cooperation by the Appellant

---

37 *Id.*, para. 15.

"could have a positive influence on the Prosecution's position in respect of a potential application for provisional release" did not amount to an inducement to the Appellant. Such a statement is clearly an inducement because it provides the incentive of a possible reward for cooperation. While cooperation with the Prosecution is not a condition of provisional release, non-cooperation is often cited by the Prosecution as a ground of opposition to an application for provisional release before the Chambers at this Tribunal. Decisions of the Appeals Chamber have made it abundantly clear that a first principle of this Tribunal is that "an accused is not required to assist the Prosecution in proving its case against them" by agreeing to be interviewed by it. Nevertheless as this case shows, the Prosecution has continued to use its influence over an application for provisional release, e.g. by not opposing or even supporting it—provided that the accused is informed in advance that such support is never binding on the competent Chamber—to persuade accused that it is in their interest to cooperate.

Accused at this Tribunal are charged with particularly serious crimes. If convicted they can expect lengthy sentences. Their trials are long and complex, and it is generally to be expected that an accused person will spend a number of years waiting for their trial to commence. Detained at The Hague, accused are often denied frequent contact with their families and friends who are financially prevented from making frequent visits from the former Yugoslavia. Taking into account the context of this Tribunal, a statement by the Prosecutor that it may not oppose an accused's application for provisional release can be a powerful incentive for an accused to speak when he may otherwise have chosen to remain silent. Accordingly, the Appeals Chamber finds that the Trial Chamber erred in finding that the statement of the Prosecution was not an inducement to the Appellant to be interviewed.

Prosecutorial offers that serve as inducements to the accused's cooperation may, if the inducement is sufficiently powerful, render statements made pursuant to that cooperation involuntary. In other cases, however, the inducement is simply an incentive;

> the fact that the accused may have taken this incentive into account when deciding whether to cooperate does not mean that the defendant was not acting voluntarily. Under the circumstances of this case, the Appeals Chamber is not satisfied that the Trial Chamber erred in finding that the statement of the Prosecution that the Appellant's cooperation "could have a positive influence on the Prosecution's position in respect of an application for provisional release" did not have the effect of rendering the Appellant's participation in the interview involuntary. While that statement may have provided an incentive to the Appellant to cooperate, it is not unreasonable to conclude that it did not have the effect of rendering that participation involuntary.
>
> However, although the Prosecution's statement may not have been of such a nature as to coerce the Appellant into cooperating with the Prosecution, it does not undermine its nature as an inducement understood as an incentive to cooperate. This was a relevant factor to be considered by the Trial Chamber in considering whether to permit the tender of the record of interview from the bar table, and the Trial Chamber erred in failing to take it into consideration when exercising its discretion to admit the record of interview.[38]

As to the potential retrial consequences of this analysis, one may conclude that it is up to the defense to establish that the particular inducement was so powerful that it resulted in an involuntary statement and that, when a conviction is (predominantly) based upon such a statement, a retrial should be allowed.

2. Procedural Safeguards to Prevent Involuntary Statements

The mentioned ICTY *Halilovic* decision of August 19, 2005, is relevant in another respect; it contemplates procedural parameters to avoid, as well as detect, involuntary statements. In this particular case, the accused put forward the argument that certain agreements were entered into with the prosecution, but the recording thereof was incomplete. The

---

38 *Id.*, paras. 35–39.

accused argued that these agreements led to his involuntary statement. The Appeals Chamber, in critically reviewing this argument, came to the following findings. First, it held that it was

> not satisfied that the Trial Chamber adequately dealt with the Appellant's claim that, prior to giving the interview, a statement was given by the Prosecution that the indictment might be withdrawn if the Appellant provided information showing that that course was warranted. In dealing with this allegation, the Trial Chamber noted that at one point in the interview the Appellant and his Defence counsel raised the issue of certain agreements reached with the Prosecutor and asked for a break in the interview in order to clarify whether those agreements reached with the Prosecution were to be respected. After the break the interview continued without any clarification on the record of what those alleged agreements were. The Trial Chamber placed no emphasis upon this break in the interview and the Appeals Chamber finds that it erred in failing to do so. The break in the record of interview indicated that the Appellant's cooperation was conditioned on his understanding that certain agreements had been reached. This break in the record and the statements made by the Appellant and his counsel prior to that break provide some support to the Appellant's argument that he would not have cooperated absent those agreements. The Appeals Chamber is satisfied that the Trial Chamber erred in failing to take this factor into account in its assessment of the voluntariness of the interview.[39]

Secondly, it held that:

> the purpose of requiring that an interview with an accused be recorded is to ensure that the accused's rights are respected at all times. Rule 43(ii) provides that, in the event of a break in the course of questioning, the fact and time of the break shall be recorded. While the Rules do not explicitly require, when an interview is stopped to address an on-the-record question of the Appellant that clearly implicates the potential non-voluntariness

---

39 *Id.*, para. 46.

> of the interview, that the parties "get an answer to the question on reached agreement so that we know how to proceed," the interview should recommence with a full explanation of what has occurred in the break and what understanding had been reached by the parties. It is only in this way that the Chamber can be satisfied that the rights of accused are in fact protected.[40]

Finally, the ICTY judges said that:

> in light of the evidence raised by the Appellant in relation to the voluntariness of the interview, it was incumbent on the Trial Chamber to fully explore the circumstances surrounding the taking of that interview. While the Trial Chamber itself did not refer to Rule 92 of the Rules it appears that the Trial Chamber was applying the principle underlying that Rule in reaching its decision. That Rule does permit the Trial Chamber to accept that a duly recorded interview with an accused is voluntary, moving the burden to establish otherwise to the accused. In this case, however, the requested break in the interview itself should have been sufficient to raise the concern of the Chamber to explore more fully the voluntariness of that interview. This does not necessarily require the holding of a *voir dire*, although there may be certain advantages in doing so.[41]

As to the potential retrial effects, it is fair to say that when the Court is heavily relying on the statement(s) of an accused, the taking of this statement should encompass an account of what was discussed during the break(s) of such an interview. In the event the accused challenges, after being convicted, the voluntariness of his statement, which led to this conviction, the absence of such a full account may constitute a potential retrial argument.

On this note, an ethically important and responsible task lies ahead for defense counsel. The ramifications of this task in the context of interviews of accused were set forth in another ICTY decision, *Prosecutor v. Jokic*, in which the admissibility of the interviews with Dragan Jokic

---

40 *Id.*, para. 41.

41 *Id.*, para. 46.

was challenged by the defense.[42] The ICTY Trial Chamber held that, "in the event that the Trial Chamber were to admit the interviews with Dragan Jokic at this stage, it would not be able to attribute much weight to this evidence and would certainly not rely on these interviews as a single source by which to determine that a given allegation has been proven beyond a reasonable doubt."[43]

The role of defense counsel in preventing involuntary statements is clearly set out in paragraph 67 of this ruling where the ICTY holds that:

> Mr. Jokic was unfamiliar with his legal rights and that is why he required legal assistance at his interviews with the Prosecution. Indeed, the purpose of Article 18(3) of the Statute and Rule 42 is not to have counsel present with a suspect during questioning but to *assist* a suspect during questioning. As it is this Trial Chamber's duty to ensure that evidence is not admitted for which the probative value is substantially outweighed by the need to ensure a fair trial, the Trial Chamber finds that, on balance, the alleged conflict of interest in relation to Mr. Jokic's counsel at the interviews, as well as the behaviour of his counsel, *may* be considered at this stage as a *contributing* factor to this Trial Chamber's decision not to admit the interviews at this stage, though it is not a sufficient reason for the Trial Chamber to deprive the Prosecution and itself of the relevant facts which may be contained in the interviews with Dragan Jokic.

In conclusion, the phenomenon of involuntary statements of accused, as defined and contemplated by the ICTY, could serve as a basis to approach this matter within domestic criminal cases, while at the same time providing grounds for potential retrials.

---

42 *See* Prosecutor v. Jokic, Decision on Prosecution's Motion for Clarification of Oral Decision regarding admissibility of accused's statement, Case No. IT-01-44, Sept. 18, 2003.

43 *Id.*, para. 69.

E. UNSAFE GUILTY PLEAS IN CRIMINAL CASES: RETRIAL GROUND ON THE BASIS OF INVESTIGATIVE MISCONDUCT

The effects of the transposition envisaged in the preceding section onto domestic criminal cases appear in a decision of the British Criminal Cases Review Commission of October 28, 2003, in the case of *Kelly and Connolly*.[44] In *Kelly and Connolly* the Court of Appeal in London held that "the scope for finding that an unequivocal and intentional plea of guilty can lead to an unsafe conviction must be exceptional and rare. However, undue pressure (. . .) or unfairness in the trial process may all be of such an important causative impact on the decision to plead guilty that the conviction which follows on such a plea can, in an appropriate case, be described as unsafe."[45]

Importantly, the Court of Appeal leaves open the possibility that violations of fair trial rights, discovered post-conviction, may invalidate a guilty plea and constitute a retrial argument.

F. CONCLUSION

In conclusion, *R. v. Ward* shows the relevance of full disclosure of medical evidence, in good faith, *vis-à-vis* the assessment of the reliability of the accused's confession. In this regard, the judgment in *R. v. Ward* of the Court of Appeal is of importance for future criminal review cases, both domestically and internationally, as it sets forth several parameters and criteria that police officials, prosecutors, and criminal courts should bear in mind with respect to the judicial evaluation of confessions made by accused persons who later claim these confessions to be untrue.

---

[44] R. Criminal Cases Review Commission, *ex* Kelly & Connolly, Case Nos. 2001/00805 S4 & 2001/03154 S4, Oct. 28, 2003, *available at* www.ccrc.gov.uk; *see*, for this Commission, Chapter 7.

[45] *Id.*, para. 127.

CHAPTER 6

MISCARRIAGES OF JUSTICE ORIGINATING FROM UNSAFE IDENTIFICATION EVIDENCE IN CRIMINAL CASES

A. THE FALLIBILITY OF "HUMAN PERCEPTION AND RECOLLECTION:" IDENTIFICATION STANDARDS OF INTERNATIONAL TRIBUNALS

In both national and international criminal cases, deficiencies in identification evidence also lead to miscarriages of justice. As far back as 1967, a U.S. court held that the "influence of improper suggestion upon identifying witnesses probably accounts for more miscarriages of justice than any other single factor; perhaps it is responsible for more errors than all other factors combined."[1] On this subject the jurisprudence of international criminal tribunals, such as the ICTY and ICTR, may be regarded as sophisticated in that it incorporates the notion of protecting against miscarriages of justice. Especially in light of the gravity of international crimes and the potential penalties at stake, international tribunals have developed important legal standards and thresholds as to the admission of identification evidence. This chapter focuses on these criteria and transposes them onto national criminal proceedings as possible protection against miscarriages of justice. In particular, the ICTY (which has in fact been influenced by several national courts) has set forth the following general parameters on identification evidence:

(1) The ICTY in *Prosecutor v. Kunarac et al.* held that identification evidence must be treated with caution due to the "many difficulties inherent in the identification process, resulting from the vagaries of human perception and recol-

1 *See* United States v. Wade, 388 U.S. 218, 228 (1967).

lection."[2] This implies that both the credibility of the witness in question and the reliability of the circumstances under which the identification took place have to be taken into account when assessing identification evidence.[3]

(2) The ICTY Appeals Chamber in *Prosecutor v. Kupreskic* indicated that Trial Chambers "must always in the interests of justice, proceed with extreme caution when assessing evidence given by a single identification witness under difficult circumstances."[4] Regard should be had to the expert testimony in the *Krupeskic* case that the relationship between the certainty conveyed by the witness and accurate identification is weak.[5]

B. RETRIAL STANDARDS WITHIN COMMON LAW

Before going into the potential retrial arguments deriving from the case law of international criminal tribunals, it is relevant to determine the requisite standards within common law. One of the leading cases in this respect is the case of *R. v. Turnbull & Others*,[6] where Lord Widgery CJ, giving the judgment of a Full Court, said:

> First, whenever the case against an accused depends wholly or substantially on the correctness of one or more identifications of the accused which the defence alleges to be mistaken, the Judge should warn the jury of the special need for caution before convicting the accused in reliance on the correctness of the identification or identifications. In addition, he should instruct them as to the reason for the need for such a warning and should make some reference to the possibility that a mistaken witness can be a convincing one and that a number of such witnesses can all be

---

2 *See* Prosecution v. Kunarac et al., Judgment, Feb. 22, 2001; *see also* Prosecutor v. Kunarac et al., Decision on Motion for Acquittal, July 3, 2000, at 8.

3 *See* Richard May & Marieke Wierda, International Criminal Evidence 175 (2002).

4 *See* Prosecutor v. Kupreskic et al., Transcripts, June 2, 1999, at 9861–2.

5 *Id.*

6 R. v. Turnbull & Others, 63 Crim. App. R. 132, para. 137.

> mistaken. Provided this is done in clear terms the Judge need not use any particular form of words.

The *Turnbull* case thus lays down three requirements at this stage of a summing up. The Judge should:

(1) Warn the jury of the special need for caution before convicting on the identification evidence;

(2) Instruct the jury as to the reason for such need; and

(3) Refer the jury to the fact that a mistaken witness can be a convincing witness and that a number of witnesses can be mistaken.

These requirements are described as "fundamental" in *R. v. Pattinson and Exley* of 1996. Lord Justice Henry said:

> So the trial Judge, in any case where the case against the accused depends wholly or substantially on identification evidence must ensure that the fundamental requirements laid down in *Turnbull* are met—and they will not be met simply by paying lip service to that judgment. This court will look to see that the message of *Turnbull* has been made clear to the jury and the reason for that was given by the Full Court in *Turnbull:* "In our judgment the dangers of miscarriage of justice occurring can be much reduced if trial judges sum up to juries in the way indicated in this judgment."[7]

This approach is reinforced by the 1999 British case of *R. v. Kamara*, in which a retrial was ordered on the basis of, *inter alia*, an unsafe conviction due to deficiencies in the identification procedure.[8] Following a reference by the Criminal Cases Review Commission (CCRC) pursuant to Section 9 of the Criminal Appeal Act 1995, the Court of Appeal, in its judgment of May 9, 2000, quashed the sentence of life imprisonment for various reasons. With respect to the identification deficiencies, it held that:

> The criticism that the Judge failed to direct the jury as to the efficacy of the parade is, we think, of more substance. The Judge referred to the recommendation of whether a separate parade

---

7 *See* 1 Crim. App. R. 51, para. 53.

8 This case is extensively discussed in Chapter 4.

should be made up of different persons, which did not happen in this case. The Judge reminded the jury of the evidence of Inspector Formby that this came about at Mr. Makin's insistence because he wanted 12 on the parade plus the suspect. The Judge said the inspector said he had no alternative but to agree.[9]

In conclusion, the common law criterion for successfully seeking a retrial based on contested identification evidence seems to be:

(1) the presence of a conviction which solely or substantially relies on identification evidence; and

(2) the presence of deficiencies of substance in the identification process.

C. RETRIAL STANDARDS BASED ON IDENTIFICATION EVIDENCE IN INTERNATIONAL CRIMINAL CASES

International tribunals have ruled on the methods and means that lead to identification evidence in practice. Two methods draw attention.

The first method is in-court or dock identifications, which in principle have been allowed by the ICTY, albeit with an evidentiary restriction. In several judgments, the ICTY has promulgated that in-court identifications have little evidentiary weight. It is felt that in-court identification is not a common procedure under international criminal law. The Trial Chamber of the ICTY has indicated that it is appropriate to "place little weight upon mere dock identification."[10] In *Prosecutor v. Tadic*, the ICTY Trial Chamber held that "the circumstances attendant upon such identification, with the accused seated between two guards in the courtroom, require the Trial Chamber to assess the credibility of each witness independently of that identification."[11]

In addition, the ICTY decision in the *Tadic* case points to another factor that may distort the reliability of in-court identifications: "The

[9] *See* R. v. Kamara, Case No. 9902769X4, Court of Appeal, May 9, 2000.

[10] *See* Prosecutor v. Jelisic, ICTY Trial Chamber, Decision on the Motion Concerning Identification Evidence of Dec. 18, 1998.

[11] *See* Prosecutor v. Tadic, ICTY Trial Chamber, Opinion and Judgment, May 7, 1997, para. 546.

potential impact of pre-trial media coverage is a factor that must be taken into account in considering the reliability of witnesses and where this aspect was raised in cross-examination of witnesses, it [must be] taken into account in the evaluation of testimony."[12]

The second method pertains to identification evidence by means of a photospread. Again, the *Tadic* decision of the ICTY is instructive. In that case, the judges accepted the photospread method as being an "unbiased identification procedure."[13] However, the judges formulated several restrictions and safeguards for this method.

(1) The "foils" in the photomap should resemble the accused. In the *Tadic* case this criterion was met. The judges (following the expert defense witness Dr. Willem A. Wagenaar) declared that the photospread "would afford witnesses a wholly *unbiased opportunity* to identify the accused, his only qualification being that the 12 men other than the accused, the 'foils,' should *prove to be of the same ethnic background as the accused* [emphasis added]. It emerged in evidence that with three exceptions this was the case; nine of the foils were from or were born in former Yugoslavia. The Trial Chamber accepts the suitability of the foils and accordingly of the photospread itself."[14]

(2) The court left open the option that "only if there were gross violations of (the) suggested (photo-spread identification) procedure . . . the identification [would] be invalid."[15] Notably, in the *Tadic* case, the photospread guidelines were not produced in evidence, and the court had to rely on the evidence given by the prosecution chief investigator, who was not present at any of the procedures but described what he had been told by the officers who had adopted the procedure. Yet this evidence was regarded by the judges as "satisfactory."

---

12 *Id.*, paras. 548–552.

13 *Id.*

14 *Id.*, para. 547.

15 *Id.*, para. 549.

(3) As noted above, the reliability of photospread identification may be negatively affected by the exposure of the witness in question to a widespread display of the accused's photo in newspapers and on television. In the *Tadic* case, however, this defense argument was rejected, in view of the convincing testimony of these witnesses that they had not seen any such media pictures of the accused before being shown the photospread. It is true that each of them knew very well that it was for the purpose of this trial that they were looking through the photospread, and that for this and other reasons, all that Dr. Wagenaar would wish by way of procedure was not complied with; for instance, the witnesses were apparently not asked in advance to give their own description of the accused so that it might be compared with the particular photograph which they selected from the photospread. However, despite what has been said to be these defects in procedure, the Trial Chamber accepts the four witnesses' identification of the accused.[16]

D. PREVENTION OF UNSAFE CONVICTIONS DUE TO IDENTIFICATION EVIDENCE IN INTERNATIONAL CRIMINAL CASES

As to specific factors that may serve as additional safeguards against miscarriages of justice originating from identification evidence, the ICTY and ICTR have developed general parameters.

In *Prosecutor v. Kupreskic et al.*, the Appeals Chamber of the ICTY, in its judgment of October 25, 2001, paragraph 40, set forth certain factors to rely upon when it concerns identification evidence in the context of unsafe convictions:

> Courts in domestic jurisdictions have identified the following factors as relevant to an appellate court's determination of whether a fact finder's decision to rely upon identification evidence was unreasonable or renders a conviction unsafe: identifications of defendants by witnesses who had only a fleeting glance or an

16 *Id.*, para. 552.

> obstructed view of the defendant; identifications occurring in the dark and as a result of a traumatic event experienced by the witness; inconsistent or inaccurate testimony about the defendant's physical characteristics at the time of the event; misidentification or denial of the ability to identify followed by later identification of the defendant by a witness; the existence of irreconcilable witness testimonies; and a witness' delayed assertion of memory regarding the defendant coupled with the "clear possibility " from the circumstances that the witness had been influenced by suggestions from others.

Another relevant factor in this regard is the relationship of the witness to the accused prior to the crime.[17] The ICTR Trial Chamber, in *Prosecutor v. Kayishema and Ruzidana*, faced with the identification of the accused at the massacre sites by prosecution witnesses, held that "the Trial Chamber is mindful of its obligation to vigorously analyse the evidence. Very pertinent is the witnesses who knew the accused prior to the massacres; identification is far more reliable when it is based upon recognition of a person already known to the witness."[18] The conditions under which such a relationship is to be established merit specific attention. In the above-mentioned ICTR decision, the judges noted:

> It is apparent that when the witnesses stated that they "knew" the accused they were not always referring to a personal acquaintance or friendship. Rather, the witnesses were sometimes referring to "knowing of" or "knowing who the accused was," due to his prominence in the community. The Trial Chamber is satisfied that the use of such phraseology was not an attempt by the witnesses to mislead the Trial Chamber. Indeed, it is consistent with common usage in much the same way as one would say that they "knew" President Nelson Mandela, even though they have only met him through his image in the media. In any event, for the purposes of identification, it is the physical recognition of the accused rather than personal acquaintance which is most pertinent. The above evidence suggests that most of the

---

17 *See* MAY & WIERDA, *supra* note 3, at 177.

18 *See* Prosecutor v. Kayishema and Ruzindana, ICTR Judgment, May 21, 1999, para. 454.

> witnesses who identified Kayishema and/or Ruzindana, were aware of the physical appearance of the accused prior to seeing them at the massacre sites.[19]

The time lapse between the events and the identification must also be taken into account. This impact on the reliability of the evidence was assessed in the ICTY *Kupreskic* case. This case involved an attack during which Bosnian Muslims were expelled from their homes by Bosnian Croats in the village of Ahmici. In paragraph 356 of the judgment, the ICTY judges observed:

> Captain Charles Stevens, the Regimental Sergeant-Major of the Cheshire Regiment, was in Ahmici some days after the massacre, and met a man who called himself "Dragan" and carried an AK47 rifle. The man indicated that he had killed 32 Muslims by drawing his hand across his throat. Captain Stevens subsequently identified Dragan Papic in court, stating that "When someone tells you they have killed 32 people, you don't forget their face in a hurry."[20]

Yet the Trial Chamber was not convinced about this identification and ruled that:

> none of the remaining prosecution evidence is sufficient to establish that Dragan Papic was an active participant in the conflict, i.e., the evidence to the effect that he was seen driving his wife and mother from his house on 15 April or that people and vehicles were gathered there that evening, or that gunfire was seen coming from his room on 16 April. As for the evidence of Captain Stevens, the Trial Chamber cannot be sure that the witness identified the correct man in court five years after the event. Therefore, the Trial Chamber finds that there is a reasonable doubt as to whether Dragan Papic participated in the conflict that day.[21]

Finally, special environmental circumstances, such as distance lighting and time span to observe the accused, may affect a witness identi-

---

19 *Id.*, para. 458.

20 *See* Prosecutor v. Kupreskic et al., ICTY Judgment, Jan. 14, 2000, para. 356.

21 *Id.*, para. 368.

fication. These issues were raised in the *Kupreskic* case. The judges dealt with them as follows:

> The Defence called a great deal of evidence to contradict the Prosecution evidence concerning the murder of Fata Pezer. Summarizing that evidence, it is convenient, first, to deal with the evidence of Professor Wagenaar, Professor of Experimental Psychology, University of Leiden, who gave his expert opinion on the identification of Vlatko Kupreskic by Witness Q. The Professor said that the important aspect of the recognition by Witness Q was the distance over which the observation was carried out. He said that, based on his studies, at the distance of 40 meters the accuracy rate is 50 per cent, i.e., it is as likely that a person would make a mistake as that they would be correct. Therefore, the likelihood of a witness making a mistake at 60 meters is higher than 50 per cent. On the other hand, matters such as the length of the observation, the fact that the person identified was in a group, and the fact that Witness Q could not provide details of clothing are not relevant since this is a case of recognition.[22]

Weighing these factors, the ICTY Trial Chamber concluded that "in the absence of confirmation of the correctness of this identification, the Trial Chamber is not able to be sure that it is correct. Accordingly, the allegation that Vlatko Kupreskic was present when these crimes were committed is not made out."[23]

The eligibility as to the occurrence of miscarriages of justice due to false eyewitness identification, is a recurring topic when dealing with war crime charges, which are frequently based on this type of evidence.[24] In the trial against ICTY accused Limaj, this issue was at stake. The ICTY, acquitting the accused, Limaj, for war crime charges allegedly committed against detainees ruled that:

> For reasons given above, the Chamber is not able to accept any of the individual identifications made by these various witnesses

---

22 *Id.*, para. 469.

23 *Id.*

24 Most of these cases can not rely on documentary evidence, such as some of the cases brought against accused before the SCSL.

> of Fatmir Limaj to be a reliable identification on the basis of which the Chamber could find beyond reasonable doubt that Fatmir Limaj was the person they saw, or knew as Çeliku, in the Llapushnik/ Lapusnik prison camp, or in the Berishe/Berisa Mountains on 25 or 26 July 1998.
>
> The Chamber has also considered the combined effect of these several identifications to determine whether they, or some of them, in combination displace the risks of mistake in the individual identifications, so as to establish beyond reasonable doubt that Fatmir Limaj was that person. While accepting that a multiplicity of identifications by a variety of persons, at different times and in different circumstances, may, in a particular case, be enough to negate the risk of honest mistake present in respect of each separate identification when it is considered separately, that is neither a common nor a simple exercise. In the present case the difficulties stipulated with respect to a number of the identifications, and the nature of the risk of mistake for each respective identification, are of such significance, in the Chamber's considered view, that, notwithstanding the strong possibility apparent on the evidence, it is on final analysis not able to be satisfied beyond reasonable doubt that Fatmir Limaj is identified to be the person referred to in their evidence by those persons, or any of them.[25]

These observations strengthen the need to scrutinize meticulously this type of evidence in order to prevent miscarriages of justice in international criminal cases.

E. CONCLUSIONS

Most international criminal trials rely upon identification evidence. While in murder cases and also war crimes cases, the admission of eyewitness identification evidence is instrumental in successfully prosecuting these crimes, at the same it exposes the criminal justice system

[25] *See* Prosecutor v. Limaj, Case No. IT-03-66, Judgment, November 30, 2005, paras. 560–561.

to the vulnerability of human perception and recollection, especially in stressful circumstances, such as violence and wars.[26] Therefore, it is of perennial concern that the fundamental safeguards, factors, and criteria as set forth in the preceding paragraph are met. Only in this way can miscarriages of justice originating from unsafe identification evidence be prevented. Conversely, these elements may be instrumental in successfully seeking a retrial.

---

[26] For this topic *see* GEERT-JAN ALEXANDER KNOOPS, THEORY AND PRACTICE OF INTERNATIONAL AND INTERNATIONALIZED CRIMINAL PROCEEDINGS 307–08 (2005).

CHAPTER 7

RETRIAL STANDARDS AND PROCEDURES IN INTERNATIONAL CRIMINAL CASES

A. INTRODUCTION

Judicial mechanisms to review and reopen criminal cases, even if ordinary procedural remedies are exhausted, are critical for the prevalence of the rule of law. This notion seems without dispute within the major legal systems of the world.[1] In order for this principle to be effective, however, it is crucial to clarify the legal prerequisites for such reopening and the legal threshold to accept reopening of a criminal case once it is closed. This issue has been the subject of legal debate both in civil and common law jurisdictions.

B. JUDICIAL REVIEW BASED ON "NEW" EVIDENCE

1. The Approach of the U.S. Supreme Court

The U.S. Supreme Court, in *Sawyer v. Whitley* (1992), held that only if new evidence has a reasonable chance in a new trial of producing a verdict of innocent and if no appeal remedy is available is a retrial justified in order to assess whether to overturn a capital conviction. The U.S. Supreme Court thus introduces a relatively high threshold for the admissibility of "new evidence" as a justification to reverse a conviction that is, in principle, irrevocable. The U.S. Supreme Court has not accepted the notion that newly discovered evidence *per se* is sufficient for judicial review of such a conviction.[2] In 1993, in *Herrera v. Collins*,

1 *See* Chapter 1.

2 *See* Sawyer v. Whitley, 505 U.S. 333 (1992); *see also* William M. Holmes,

the U.S. Supreme Court somewhat refined this approach, holding that "a truly persuasive demonstration of actual innocence" would render conviction unconstitutional.[3] As a result, according to U.S. case law, the burden rests on the convicted to establish that he or she has a reasonable case of proving innocence.[4] Accordingly, two guidelines can be derived from the U.S. Supreme Court approach:

(1) The newly introduced evidence must be "truly persuasive" as to factual innocence; and

(2) It must be established that this new evidence was unavailable at the time of the initial conviction.

Hence, within the U.S. system, it does not suffice that the accused merely asserts wrongful conviction. On the other hand, what "new evidence" exactly is, or what the criterion "truly persuasive" encompasses, remains unclear. One may ask what the difference is between "truly persuasive" and merely "persuasive" new evidence. The nature and content of what qualifies as "new evidence" that meets the "persuasiveness" test must be determined on a case-by-case basis. A survey of existing U.S. case law on review cases reveals that U.S. judges interpret these criterion relatively strictly.

2. The Approach of U.K. Courts and the British Criminal Cases Review Commission (CCRC)

a. Toward a New Perception of Miscarriages of Justice: The *Birmingham Six* Precedents

The United Kingdom appears to have a more extensive and teleological view on the nature and scope of "new evidence" that can justify a retrial.

The Birmingham Six and *Guildford Four* cases represent pressing examples of miscarriages of justice. In the *Birmingham Six* case, the ini-

---

Who Are the Wrongly Convicted on Death Row?, *in* WRONGLY CONVICTED: PERSPECTIVES ON FAILED JUSTICE 101 (Saundra D. Westervelt & John A. Humphrey eds., 2001).

3 *See* Herrera v. Collins, 506 U.S. 390 (1993).

4 *See* Holmes, *supra* note 2, at 101.

tial convictions were quashed in 1991 by the Court of Appeal, after the accuseds had spent approximately 16 years in prison. The defendants in the *Guildford Four* case saw their convictions overturned by the Court of Appeal in October 1989, after being detained over 14 years. Both cases arose out of the IRA bombing campaign in the United Kingdom in 1974. Notably, police and prosecutors at the time were under considerable public pressure to bring those responsible to justice, a factor that is known to increase the risk of a wrongful conviction.[5] These cases offer clear examples of false confessions based both on psychological and physical pressure and tampering with accused's interview records.

The Guildford Four all wrote self-incriminating confessions, which they subsequently retracted and alleged were made under duress. Four of the Birmingham Six made written confessions, two did not. All of the Birmingham Six alleged that they were extensively physically threatened and assaulted during their custodial interrogation in 1974. The Guildford Four have alleged also physical threats and assaults, albeit of lesser severity than those reported by the Birmingham Six. Whereas the Guildford Four were convicted on the basis of uncorroborated confessions, forensic science evidence was presented against two of the Birmingham Six, evidence that has subsequently been totally discredited.[6]

The *Birmingham Six* case also highlights the risk inherent in overestimating the role of forensic science in criminal cases. In that case, a forensic scientist conducted two tests for the presence of nitroglycerine on the hands of the accuseds. The first test had a positive result for the hands of accuseds A and B. Yet, negative results emerged for accuseds C, D, E and F. Subsequently, a second test, reportedly a thousand times more sensitive, resulted in a different outcome: a negative result was established for A and B, but a positive result for C. From a forensic sciences perspective, these tests, seen all together, did not accumulate conclusive data that warranted any deduction on the purported guilt of the accuseds. However, the forensic expert informed the court otherwise. The first test, he testified in court, made him 99 percent certain that the

---

5 *See* Chapter 3.

6 For these cases *see* GISLI H. GUDJONSSON, THE PSYCHOLOGY OF INTERROGATIONS, CONFESSIONS AND TESTIMONY 272–73 (1993).

accused had been in contact with nitroglycerine, whereas the second test made him, as he stated, 100 percent certain.[7]

Following several pertinent miscarriages of justice, i.e., *Birmingham Six, Guildford Four*, and *Maguire Seven*,[8] the British Home Office, in March 1997, vested an independent institution, the Criminal Cases Review Commission (CCRC), to investigate claims of innocence. The CCRC was established in response to calls for a new mechanism for redressing possible miscarriages of justice. Before it was established, the procedure for considering whether a particular conviction ought to be referred back to the Court of Appeal called for an application to the Home Office for consideration by officials as to whether it should be brought before the Home Secretary. To many observers, this procedure was unacceptably slow and insufficiently independent, and delivered too many wrong decisions. As far back as 1976, Lord Devlin, in a Report on Evidence of Identification in Criminal Cases, had raised the idea that there should be a new body, independent of the Home Secretary, which would take such decisions. In 1982, the then Home Affairs Committee had made recommendations along similar lines, but these recommendations were not accepted by the then government.

b. The Inception of a Specialized Investigative Body for Review Cases

During the 1980s, cases where persons had been wrongly convicted continued to come to prominence in the United Kingdom. In March 1991, on the day that the Court of Appeal quashed convictions for murder in the *Birmingham Six* case, the establishment of a Royal Commission on Criminal Justice, chaired by Lord Runciman, was announced. The Royal Commission was given wide-ranging terms of reference to examine the various stages of the criminal justice process, including "the arrangements for considering and investigating allegations of miscarriage of justice when appeal rights have been exhausted."

---

7 *See* Spencer, *supra* note 7.

8 *See* McIlkenny et al., 93 Crim. App. R. 289, 296 (1991); *see* John R. Spencer, *Evidence and Forensic Science, in* HARMONISATION IN FORENSIC EXPERTISE 551 (J.F. Nijboer & W.J.J.M. Sprangers eds., 2000).

The Royal Commission reported in July 1993. Among many other proposed criminal justice reforms, it recommended the abolition of the Home Secretary's power to refer cases back to the Court of Appeal and the establishment of a new body, independent of government, which would be charged with receiving applications and considering whether they should be referred back to the Court of Appeal. This recommendation was accepted by the then government, and the new body was established under Part II of the Criminal Appeal Act 1995, as the Criminal Cases Review Commission (CCRC). The Royal Commission's remit covered England, Wales, and Northern Ireland; similar legislation establishing a separate body for Scotland followed in due course.

i. The CCRC's Procedures[9]

Apart from the ongoing cases, which were transferred from the Home Office and the Northern Ireland Office, the review process begins when an application is received. Most applicants (around 80 percent) are not legally represented at this point, and the application can come in any form.

ii. Stage 1: Initial Assessment

The application is then subjected to what the Commission terms a "Stage 1" examination by a small team of Commission staff specifically allocated to this role. This stage involves an initial assessment as to whether the application is eligible for review by the Commission. Most cases have been rejected as ineligible, often because the normal appeal process has not yet been exhausted. Eligible cases are passed on to the Commission's "Stage 2" for substantive review.

During the Stage 1 initial assessment, staff also take the necessary steps to obtain the basic required documentation and arrange for directions to be issued under Section 17 or Section 18 of the Act to ensure that papers relating to the case are preserved by the relevant authorities. A preliminary assessment is also made at this stage for those cases that

[9] This text is adapted from http://www.parliament.the-stationery-office.co.uk/pa/cm199899/cmselect/cmnaff/106/10602.htm.

are eligible for review of whether grounds exist for the case to be given any special priority. A judgment will also be made of whether the application appears to be one that, though eligible for review, contains no ground on which it is likely to succeed even if the allegations contained in the application are found to be true; such cases will be passed on to Stage 2, which is the stage at which the main review of all eligible applications takes place, but with a recommendation that it receive only an abbreviated review, the so-called "short form of review."

iii. Stage 2: Substantive Review

At Stage 2, a Case Review Manager (or "caseworker") and a Commission member are assigned to work on the case. The caseworker prepares a case action plan and discusses this with the assigned Commission member. The caseworker is in charge of going through all the documentation, making all the necessary inquiries (or arranging for them to be made), and (with the assigned Commission member) coming to a preliminary view on whether the case should be referred back to the Court of Appeal. When this process is judged to be complete, the case is put to a panel of three members of the Commission, who will decide whether the case should be referred back or the application rejected. If the application is one that has been assessed as suitable for the accelerated short form of review procedure, it will be subjected to a briefer review and put for decision for rejection by a single Commission member; however, at any stage in this accelerated procedure, a decision can be made that the case should, after all, be subjected to the full review process.

iv. Stage 3: Appointment of an Investigating Officer

In a small number of cases a decision is taken that the inquiries, which need to be made, are such that there is a need for an outside investigation. The Commission can then appoint an "investigating officer"—generally though not necessarily a police officer—under Section 19 of the Act. The Commission refers to this part of the process as "Stage 3."

c. The CCRC Review System

Convicts may, after closure of a criminal case, petition the CCRC in order to obtain a retrial before a Court of Appeal.

Notably, the CCRC, staffed by former prosecutors, judges and defense lawyers, may grant a retrial based upon new evidence and new arguments.[10] The latter retrial ground also permits new defenses, which were not raised during the trial proceedings and which exceed existence of new evidence; for instance, an accused was not able to invoke the argument of self-defense due to the absence of evidence thereto, while such evidence (for example, a material witness who supports the self-defense claim) emerges only after conviction. Under the CCRC system, such a situation may justify a retrial.[11]

The British review system was aptly explained in *R. v. Criminal Case Review Commission ex parte M. Pearson*, judgment of May 18, 1999, rendered by the Court of Appeal. In paragraphs 9–15, the Lord Chief Justice sets forth as follows:

> The expression "unsafe" in section 2(1)(a) of the 1968 Act does not lend itself to precise definition. In some cases unsafety will be obvious, as (for example) where it appears that someone other than the appellant committed the crime and the appellant did not, or where the appellant has been convicted of an act that was not in law a crime, or where a conviction is shown to be vitiated by serious unfairness in the conduct of the trial or significant legal misdirection, or where the jury verdict, in the context of other verdicts, defies any rational explanation. Cases however arise in which unsafety is much less obvious: cases in which the court, although by no means persuaded of an appellant's innocence, is subject to some lurking doubt or uneasiness whether an injustice has been done (*R v. Cooper* [1969] 1 QB 267 at 271). If, on consideration of all the facts and circumstances of the case before it, the court entertains real doubts whether the appellant was guilty of the offence of which he has been convicted, the

10 *See* for the interpretation of these criteria the Pearson case discussed below.

11 *See* Section B.4.

court will consider the conviction unsafe. In these less obvious cases the ultimate decision of the Court of Appeal will very much depend on its assessment of all the facts and circumstances.

So far as relevant to this application, section 23 of the 1968 Act now provides:

> "(1) For the purposes of an appeal under this Part of this Act the Court of Appeal may, if they think it necessary or expedient in the interests of justice— . . .
>
> > "(c) receive any evidence which was not adduced in the proceedings from which the appeal lies.
>
> "(2) The Court of Appeal shall, in considering whether to receive any evidence, have regard in particular to—
>
> > "(a) whether the evidence appears to the Court to be capable of belief;
> >
> > "(b) whether it appears to the Court that the evidence may afford any ground for allowing the appeal;
> >
> > "(c) whether the evidence would have been admissible in the proceedings from which the appeal lies on an issue which is the subject of the appeal; and
> >
> > "(d) whether there is a reasonable explanation for the failure to adduce the evidence in those proceedings."

This power has evolved over the years. In section 9 of the Criminal Appeal Act of 1907 the Court of Criminal Appeal was empowered to receive new evidence if the Court thought it necessary or expedient in the interest of justice. By section 5 of the Criminal Appeal Act 1966, this power of the Court to receive fresh evidence became a duty if certain conditions were satisfied:

> "Without prejudice to the generality of section 9 of the 1907 Act (supplemental powers), where evidence is tendered to the Court of Appeal under that section, the Court shall, unless they are satisfied that the evidence if received would not afford any ground for allowing the appeal, exercise their powers under that section of receiving it if—

> "(a) it appears to them that the evidence is likely to be credible and would have been admissible at the trial on an issue which is the subject of the appeal; and
>
> "(b) they are satisfied that it was not adduced at the trial, but that there is a reasonable explanation for the failure so to adduce it."

As originally enacted in the 1968 Act, section 23 again conferred a general power to receive fresh evidence if the Court thought it necessary or expedient in the interests of justice, and also a mandatory duty to receive such evidence subject to the conditions in section 5 of the 1966 Act, reproduced in section 23(2) of the 1968 Act. Under section 23 as it now stands, it is plain that the Court of Appeal has a discretion to receive evidence not adduced in the trial court if the court think it necessary or expedient in the interests of justice to receive it. The Court of Appeal is never subject to a mandatory duty to receive the evidence, but is bound in considering whether to receive the evidence or not to have regard in particular to the specific matters listed in subsection (2). The Court of Appeal is not precluded from receiving fresh evidence if the conditions in subsection (2)(a), (b), (c) and (d) or any of them are not satisfied, but the Court would for obvious reasons be unlikely to receive evidence which did not appear to it to afford any ground for allowing the appeal, or which would not have been admissible in the trial court. The Court of Appeal would ordinarily be less ready, and in some cases much less ready, to receive evidence which the appellant had failed without reasonable explanation to adduce at the trial, since receipt of such evidence on appeal tends to subvert our system of jury trial by depriving the decision-making tribunal of the opportunity to review and assess the strength of that fresh evidence in the context of the case as a whole, and retrials, although sometimes necessary, are never desirable. On any application to the Court of Appeal to receive fresh evidence under section 23 in an appeal against conviction, the question which the Court of Appeal must always ask itself is this: having regard in particular to the matters listed in subsection (2), does the Court of Appeal think it necessary or expedient in the interests of justice to receive the new evidence? In exercising its statutory discretion to receive or not to receive fresh evidence, the Court of Appeal will be mindful that its discretion is to be exercised in accordance with the statutory provision and so as to achieve, in the infinitely varying circumstances of different cases, the objective for which the discretion has been conferred. The exercise of this discretion cannot be circumscribed in a manner which fails to give effect to the statute or undermines the statutory objective, which is to promote the interests of justice; the Court will bear in mind that the power in section 23 exists to safeguard defendants against the risk and consequences of wrongful conviction.

The power to order retrial was first conferred on the Court of Appeal by section 1 of the Criminal Appeal Act 1964, but the power was only exercisable where an appeal against conviction was allowed by reason only of the reception or availability of fresh evidence. This provision was re-enacted in 1968, but was amended by section 43 of the Criminal Justice 1988 so as to remove the restriction of the power to fresh evidence cases. The Court of Appeal is now readier to order retrials than it was.

The Criminal Appeal Act 1995 abolished the power of the Secretary of State to refer case for reconsideration by the Court of Appeal, and created the Commission. This was to be a body of not fewer than 11 members, of whom at least one third were to be legally qualified and at least two thirds to have knowledge or experience of the criminal justice system. The procedure of the Commission by paragraph 6(1) of Schedule 1 to the Act, was to be such as it might determine. By section 9 of the Act, the Commission was empowered to refer to the Court of Appeal the conviction of any person convicted of an offence on indictment in England and Wales, and such a reference was to be treated by the Court for all purposes as an appeal by the defendant against conviction under the 1968 Act. Section 13 of the Act prescribes the conditions for making references. In the case of a conviction, the section provides:

"(1) A reference of a conviction . . . shall not be made under any of sections 9 10 12 unless—

> "(a) the Commission consider that there is a real possibility that the conviction . . . would not be upheld were the reference to be made,
>
> (b) the Commission so consider—
>
> "(i) in the case of a conviction . . . because of an argument, or evidence not raised in the proceedings which led to it or on any appeal or application for leave to appeal against it . . . and
>
> "(c) an appeal against the conviction . . . has been determined or leave to appeal against it has been refused.
>
> "(2) Nothing in subsection (1)(b)(i) or (c) shall prevent the making of a reference if it appears to the Commission that there are exceptional circumstances which justify making it.

Thus the Commission's power to refer under section 9 is exercisable only if it considers that if the reference were made there would be a real possibility that the conviction would not be upheld by the Court of Appeal. The exercise of the power to refer accordingly depends on the judgment of the Commission, and it cannot be too strongly emphasised that this is a judgment entrusted to the Commission and to no one else. Save in exceptional circumstances, the judgment must be made by the Commission, in a conviction case, on the ground of an argument or evidence which has not been before the court before, whether at trial, on application for leave to appeal or on appeal. In the absence of such exceptional circumstances, the Commission cannot therefore invite the court to review issues or evidence upon which there has already been a ruling. Resort to the Commission must ordinarily follow and not precede resort to the Court of Appeal.

The "real possibility" test prescribed in section 13(1)(a) of the 1995 Act as the threshold which the Commission must judge to be crossed before a conviction may be referred to the Court of Appeal is imprecise but plainly denotes a contingency which, in the Commission's judgment, is more than an outside chance or a bare possibility but which may be less than a probability or a likelihood or a racing certainty. The Commission must judge that there is at least a reasonable prospect of a conviction, if referred, not being upheld. The threshold test is carefully chosen: if the Commission were almost automatically to refer all but the most obviously threadbare cases, its function would be mechanical rather than judgmental and the Court of Appeal would be burdened with a mass of hopeless appeals; if, on the other hand, the Commission were not to refer any case unless it judged the applicant's prospect of success on appeal to be assured, the cases of some deserving applicants would not be referred to the Court and the beneficial object which the Commission was established to achieve would be to that extent defeated. The commission is entrusted with the power and the duty to judge which cases cross the threshold and which do not.

The judgment required of the Commission is a very unusual one, because it inevitably involves a prediction of the view which another body (the Court of Appeal) may take. In a case which is likely to turn on the willingness of the Court of Appeal to receive fresh evidence, the Commission must also make a judgment how, on all the facts of a given case, the Court of Appeal is likely to resolve an application to adduce that evidence under section 23, because there could in such a case be no real possibility that the conviction would not be upheld were the reference to be made unless there were also a real possibility that the Court of Appeal would receive the evidence in question. Thus, in a conviction case of this kind, the first task of the Commission is to judge whether there is a real possibility that the court of Appeal would receive the evidence. The Commission has, in effect, to predict how the Court of Appeal is likely to answer the question which arises under section 23, as formulated above. In a conviction case depending on the reception of fresh evidence, the Commission must ask itself a double question: do we consider that there is a real possibility that the Court of Appeal will receive the fresh evidence? If so, do we consider that there is a real possibility that the court of Appeal will not uphold the conviction? The Commission would not in such a case refer unless it gave an affirmative answer to both questions. The parties are

> agreed, and we accept, that the test of "real possibility" is the appropriate test in asking both questions and not only the question arising under section 13(1)(a).[12]

Overviewing the U.K. review system of criminal cases, one can say that it provides a meticulous and independent system of both procedural and substantive guarantees against miscarriages of justice—a system that certainly may serve as an example for other jurisdictions both nationally and internationally. Instead of promulgating a rigid system of rules, it heavily relies on moral-ethical notions and on justice. In particular, the "real possibility" test, as defined by the *Pearson* decision, creates a practical and justifiable avenue to redress wrongful convictions.

3. The Approach of the Dutch Supreme Court

This section now arrives at an assessment of the requisite retrial standard within a civil law system, i.e., the view of the Dutch Supreme Court. The statutory provision within the Dutch Code of Criminal Proceedings, Article 457, Section 1(2), enables a retrial based on a "new fact" (a *"novum"*) such that the trial judges who convicted the accused, in the event they would have been familiar with this particular fact, "most likely" would have brought in an acquittal of the accused. As in the U.S. system, any definition of this criterion "new fact" is absent. The legal contours of this element are yet to be developed by the case law of the Dutch Supreme Court, the highest judicial body of the land, which holds exclusive competence to adjudicate requests for retrials. Like the U.S. Supreme Court, the Dutch Supreme Court has set a relatively high and strict standard for the admission of a "new fact." According to this Court, a new fact should fulfill the condition of a new piece of evidence in a factual sense, which likely would have resulted in an acquittal at the initial trial, given that this fact was not known to the judges who rendered the initial conviction. This new fact must be irreconcilable with the conviction. Finally, a mere opinion or conclusion of a new expert witness is, in principle, not sufficient to meet this criterion, unless the expert

12 *See* R. v. Criminal Cases Review Commission *Ex parte* Pearson [1999] Crim. L.R. 1999, Sept., 732–34, paras. 9–15.

witness evidence is based on new factual circumstances that were unknown to both the expert and the judges during the original criminal proceedings.[13]

The Dutch Supreme Court has created the following judicial guidelines for review cases on the basis of new forensic evidence. A new opinion by an expert witness can be admitted as a new fact, justifying the reopening of a criminal case, contingent upon the following three criteria:

(1) It should be established that the Court of Appeal came to the initial conviction based upon its belief that the facts of the case permitted a certain course of events;

(2) It should be established that the Court of Appeal could only have deduced this course of events from the opinion of an expert witness heard during the initial criminal proceedings; and

(3) At the basis for a review request should be the opinion of the particular expert witness, which now qualifies the initial course of events as highly improbable.[14]

Whether other exceptional circumstances may justify the reopening of a criminal case remains open. In examining the jurisprudence of the Dutch Supreme Court, other circumstances are conceivable presupposing that the expert opinion featured prominently within the direct evidence adduced by the prosecution and accepted by the Court. Here the Dutch Supreme Court seems to pursue the criterion that expert evidence was directly related to the evidence that led to the conviction.

4. Retrial Standards Before the International Criminal Tribunals

After examining how domestic criminal jurisdictions perceive the element of "new evidence" as a justification for a retrial, it is important to address this element from the perspective of the international criminal tribunals. As these systems are predominantly based on a mixture of common and civil law traits,[15] their approach to retrial proceedings may help to set standards in a wide range of national retrial proceedings.

---

13 *See* Judgment Dutch Supreme Court NJ 2001 564, June 26, 2001.

14 *Id.*

15 *See* William A. Schabas, An Introduction to the International Criminal Court 94–96 (2001).

a. ICTY-ICTR Criteria

The fact that trials may not be perfect and are thus vulnerable to miscarriages of justice is acknowledged in both the ICTY (Article 26) and ICTR (Article 25) Statutes. The possibility of moving for review of the Trial Chamber's or the Appeals Chamber's judgment is not unlimited, however. ICTY Rule 119 and ICTR Rule 120 provide that "where a new fact has been discovered which was not known to the moving party at the time of the proceedings before a Trial Chamber or the Appeals Chamber, and could not have been discovered through the exercise of due diligence, the defense or, within one year after the final judgement has been pronounced, the Prosecutor, may make motion to that Chamber for review of the judgment." At first sight, three objective criteria emerge from this rule:

(1) The existence of a new fact;

(2) The moving party was not familiar with this new fact and this fact could not have been discovered through the exercise of due diligence; and

(3) Unlike the defense, the prosecutor is obliged to make a motion for review within one year after the final judgment.

The criterion of "a new fact" must not be confused with the power to present additional evidence, which was not available to a party at the trial (Rule 115 of the ICTY RPE), or the power attributed to the Appeals Chamber to admit relevant or probative evidence, which was not litigated before the Trial Chamber pursuant to Rule 107.

As to the distinction between an application according to Rule 115 and a new fact for review under Rule 119, the ICTY Appeals Chamber drew a clear line in the *Tadic* case: "Where an applicant seeks to present a new fact which becomes known only after trial, despite the exercise of due diligence during the trial in discovering it, Rule 119 is the governing provision. In such a case, the Appellant is not seeking to admit additional evidence of a fact that was considered at trial, but rather a new fact. The proper venue for a review application is the Chamber that rendered the final judgment; it is to that Chamber that the motion for review should be made."[16]

---

[16] *See* Prosecutor v. Tadic, Decision on Appellant's Motion for the Extension of the Time-Limit and Admission of Additional Evidence, Oct. 15, 1998, para. 30.

b. ICTY-ICTR Case Law on Review Proceedings

Thus far, a review procedure pursuant to Rule 119 has been followed once and once only in ICTY-ICTR practice: before the ICTR Appeals Chamber in *Prosecutor v. Barayagwiza*. Review was sought by the prosecutor from the original Appeals Chamber judgment of November 3, 1999, which had resulted in a dismissal of the charges with prejudice and release of the accused due to severe prosecutorial inaction and repeated infringement of the fundamental rights of the accused.[17] Bearing in mind the first and second conditions of Rule 119, the prosecutor emphasized the presence of new facts that could have been decisive elements in the initial judgment of November 3, 1999, in view of the element that these were not known at that stage of the proceedings. The prosecutor's reasoning was that the Appeals Chamber, in its initial proceedings, did not inform the parties that it would render its decision on the basis of the abuse of process doctrine. Had the prosecution been familiar with this starting point, it would have been able to present the Chamber with new facts demonstrating that the violation of fundamental defense rights had not been as serious as the original Appeals Chamber had qualified them. The ICTR Appeals Chamber granted the review request, holding that these facts could not have been known to the prosecutor by means of exercising due diligence.[18] Although it can be questioned whether this interpretation of the judicial term "new fact" overstretches the rationale of Rule 119, this judgment of March 31, 2000, is important to further develop review proceedings before the ICTR as it delineates four criteria applicable to review proceedings:

(1) The presence of a new fact;

(2) This new fact must not have been known by the moving party at the time of the initial proceedings;

(3) The lack of discovery of the new fact must not have occurred through absence of due diligence on part of the applicant; and

---

[17] *See* Prosecutor v. Barayagwiza, Appeals Chamber Decision, Nov. 3, 1999, para. 106.

[18] *See* Prosecutor v. Barayagwiza, Appeals Chamber Decision Mar. 31, 2000, on Prosecutor's Request for Review or Reconsideration, para. 31.

(4) It must be probable that the new fact could have been a decisive factor in rendering the initial decision.[19]

c. ICTR's Extensive View on the "New Fact" Criterion

Analysis of this case law reveals two additional observations as to the exact scope of the first criterion, namely the requisite element of a "new fact."

First, the Appeals Chamber in *Prosecutor v. Barayagwiza* held that a "fact" can be seen as "new" even if the event to which it relates occurred before the trial.[20] Indeed, the ICTR Appeals Chamber endorses a rather extensive and teleological view "by asking itself whether the fact was new in relation to the facts previously before the Court."[21] This implies that the alleged new fact is subjected to a contextual interpretation as well as to a balancing operation between the existing evidence, on the one hand, and the intensity and newness of the presented fact, on the other.[22]

Second, the ICTR Appeals Chamber is apparently willing to accept a fact as "new" in terms of Rule 119, even if the applicant must have been familiar with a part of that fact. This may be concluded from paragraph 65 of the *Barayagwiza* judgment of March 31, 2000, which reads:

> In the wholly exceptional circumstances of this case, and in the face of a possible miscarriage of justice, the Chamber construes the condition laid down in Rule 120, that the fact be unknown to the moving party at the time of the proceedings before a Chamber, and not discoverable through the exercise of due diligence, as directory in nature . . . To reject the facts presented by the Prosecutor, in the light of their impact on the Decision, would indeed be to close one's eyes to reality.[23]

---

19 *See* RICHARD MAY & MARIEKE WIERDA, INTERNATIONAL CRIMINAL EVIDENCE 316 (2002).

20 *See* Prosecutor v. Barayagwiza, *supra* note 18, para. 44.

21 *See* MAY & WIERDA, *supra* note 19, at 316; *see* Prosecutor v. Barayagwiza, *supra* note 18, paras. 54, 57, 61.

22 *See also* Separate Opinion of Judge Shahabuddeen to the *Barayagwiza* decision, *supra* note 18, para. 56.

23 *See* MAY & WIERDA, *supra* note 19, at 317.

Indeed, bearing this paragraph in mind, the conclusion of some commentators seems justified, namely that "the Appeals Chamber may be ultimately willing to consider facts that come to its attention, even if they are not new, if their impact is such as to reverse a miscarriage of justice."[24] Therefore, in exceptional circumstances, the Appeals Chamber finds that an exception is justified in deviating from the above-mentioned criteria (2) and/or (3) when the interests of justice so require. This may be the case when it is likely that a miscarriage of justice is at stake, which can be reversed. This view is also aptly envisioned by Judge Shahabuddeen in his Separate Opinion to the *Barayagwiza* Appeals Chamber's decision of March 31, 2000, in which he says: "Thus, there has to be recognition of the possibility of there being a case in which, notwithstanding the absence of diligence, the material in question is so decisive in demonstrating mistake that the court in its discretion is obliged to admit it in the upper interests of justice."[25]

In conclusion, it is fair to say that this extensive and teleological interpretation of Rule 119 of the ICTY RPE (Rule 120 of the ICTR RPE) is reasonable, albeit in special circumstances, bearing in mind that the *rationale* of a review possibility is ultimately to serve as a final opportunity to avoid or redress any possible miscarriage of justice.[26]

d. The Revision System Under the ICC Statute

Revision of conviction or sentence is dealt with in Article 84 of the ICC Statute in greater detail than it is in the relevant articles of the ICTY and ICTR Statutes. Within the framework of the ICC Statute, the procedural conditions for revision are threefold:

(1) the discovery of new evidence, which likely would have resulted in "a different verdict;"

(2) the new discovery that decisive evidence, used during the trial and relevant to the conviction, was false, forged or falsified; or

---

24 *Id.*

25 *See* Prosecutor v. Barayagwiza, *supra* note 18, para. 50.

26 See MAY & WIERDA, *supra* note 19, at 317.

(3) the finding that during the conviction or confirmation of the charges in the case in question, the presiding judge was implicated in and guilty of serious misconduct or serious breach of duty, sufficient to justify removal from the bench.

C. THE DETERMINATION AND STANDARD OF "NEW EVIDENCE" IN CRIMINAL CASES: TOWARD A UNIFORM MODEL

The preceding section raises the question as to what exactly constitutes "new evidence" in order to petition for a retrial. In other words, is there a common standard to determine the existence of "new evidence?" In this connection, the case law of the British Criminal Cases Review Commission (CCRC) may be seen as authoritative, particularly in light of its specialized and professional engagement in the area of miscarriages of justice, such that its precedents can be transposed to other criminal law systems and even those of the international criminal tribunals. In this regard, the following scheme or model, derived from the CCRC decisions, can be functional.

In addition to the criteria set forth by the *Pearson* decision,[27] the decision of the CCRC in the *Pendleton* case merits attention. In this case, for new evidence to be accepted, the CCRC promulgated the test to be met: "The test is what impact the evidence, if called at the trial, might have had on the jury."[28] This criterion can be transferred also to the reliance on new evidence before professional judges panels.

As to the level of impact to be required in this respect, the ruling in the *McNamee* case is instructive. In that case, McNamee was convicted for complicity in a bomb attack, which conviction mainly relied on his thumbprint on a bomb fragment. In 1997, the CCRC referred his case to the Court of Appeal, which, in 1998, overturned the conviction, since new forensic evidence revealed that the particular fingerprint could not be conclusively matched with McNamee's prints. The "impact" of new evidence is defined by the Court of Appeal as follows: "The impact of the fresh evidence on the case is not conclusive, but it is such as to ren-

---

27 *See* Section B.2.b for this case.

28 R. v. Criminal Cases Review Commission, *ex* Pendleton, 2001 U.K.H.L. 66, para. 12.

der the verdict of the jury unsafe because a reasonable tribunal of fact might properly resolve the conflict in favour of the Appellant, and so be left with a reasonable doubt as to his guilt."[29] The exact criterion is thus that of a "reasonable tribunal of fact" that should be left with "a reasonable doubt as to (the) guilt." This approach is tantamount to a "double test of reasonableness" that should be applied in order to admit new evidence for the purpose of reviewing criminal cases.

Another element in this model involves the position of the new evidence within the composition of the prosecution case as a whole. This element was clearly formulated in the *Rowe* case brought before the CCRC, in which it was held that "the fresh evidence, although relevant and credible, adds so little to the weight of the defence case as compared with the weight of the prosecution case that a doubt induced by the fresh evidence would not be a reasonable doubt, so we leave the conviction standing, and dismiss the appeal."[30]

D. JUDICIAL REVIEW BASED ON "NEW" DEFENSES OR ARGUMENTS

A principal question is whether criminal cases may be reviewed and reopened on the basis of "new" defenses or arguments that were not raised during the initial trial. Unlike most civil law systems, the British judicial review system, as noticed above, opens the possibility that a retrial can be granted on the basis of such a defense or argument *de novo*. The following examples illustrate this legal avenue.

The 1996 case of *R. v. Arnold* is often cited as authoritative in this regard. This case concerned a 50-year-old schoolteacher who had been convicted of murdering another woman and her eight-month-old baby. At her trial, she had denied any connection with the killings, without success. The Court of Appeal observed that on the issues contested at the trial, there was clearly nothing unsafe about the verdict. After conviction, the appellant was confined in prison, then in a regional secure unit where she received psychiatric help, and then at Broadmoor. At

---

29 *See* R. v. Criminal Cases Review Commission, *ex* McNamee, Case No. 9704481 S2, Dec. 17, 1998, *available at* www.ccrc.gov.uk.

30 *See* R. v. Criminal Cases Review Commission, *ex* Rowe, Case No. 99/6552/Z4, Dec. 8, 2000, *available at* www.ccrc.gov.uk.

Broadmoor a consultant forensic psychiatrist suggested that there were psychological grounds for contesting the appellant's conviction, and other expert opinions to the same effect were obtained. Application was then made to adduce this evidence in the Court of Appeal and to seek substitution of convictions of manslaughter on grounds of diminished responsibility for the conviction of murder. Giving the judgment of the court, Hobhouse L.J. said:

> On this appeal, the critical question is whether we accede to the application of the appellant under section 23 that new evidence should be received. Without the new evidence the appellant has no ground of appeal. However, the criteria which the Court has to consider in exercising its discretion under section 23 as now amended overlap with a consideration of the cogency of the proposed evidence and whether it would lead to the conclusion that the convictions were unsafe.[31]

The Court went on to observe that the decision whether to raise the defense of diminished responsibility was one for the defense at the trial and not the Court of Appeal.[32] Having recited the terms of Section 23 as amended, the Court continued:

> The discretion of the Court of Appeal is thus unfettered—as it was under subsection (1) of the original section 23. The revised wording of subsection (2) preserves the breadth of this discretion whilst at the same time directing the Court to have particular regard to the matters listed under paragraphs (a) to (d) when deciding how to exercise its discretion. It is not fatal to an appellant's application that the Court receive new evidence that the issue to which it is relevant was not raised at the trial; it, however, remains a factor to be taken into consideration. Similarly the Court must consider what, if any, reasonable explanation there is for the failure to adduce the evidence at the trial. Ultimately, the most important consideration must always be whether the proffered evidence may afford a ground for allow-

31 *See* R. v. Arnold (CACD, unreported, Feb. 7, 1996) cited in paras. 29–30 of the *Pearson* decision of the U.K. Divisional court of May 18, 1999, which is described at Section B.2.c.

32 *Id.* at 22.

> ing the appeal. If it does not, it is unlikely to be necessary or expedient in the interests of justice that the evidence should be received. The evidence must provide a basis for a conclusion that the conviction of the appellant was unsafe.[33]

Having cited the observations of Lord Taylor C.J. in *R. v. Ahluwalia* on the importance of advancing any available defense at trial, and making reference to *R. v. Dodd, R. v. Melville*, and *R. v. Richardson*, the Court turned to the new evidence upon which the appellant sought to rely. In the Court's judgment, certain facts were fatal to the application, namely that, by the time of trial, all the material relevant to the defense of diminished responsibility had been available; that the medical opinions inevitably depended on the factual evidence of the appellant; and that she had throughout been unwilling to provide an adequate account of the facts on which such opinions could be based. In its conclusions the Court said:

> We come back to the factors which the Court is required to take into account in deciding whether it considers it necessary or expedient in the interest of justice to accede to the application under section 23. They can be taken in reverse order.
>
> Yet, no reasonable explanation for the failure to adduce evidence of diminished responsibility at the trial has been given. The only conclusion which we can draw is that such a defence was considered at the time of preparing for the trial; that there was then available psychiatric evidence, which does not materially differ from the psychiatric evidence now available, to support the defence if the factual basis was laid. The present case falls fairly and squarely within the observations of Lord Taylor C.J. already quoted from *Ahluwalia*.
>
> The evidence now tendered from Professor Bluglass and Dr. Dilys Jones would not be admissible in the form in which it is tendered to us because it expresses opinions based upon facts which are not in evidence. This is a case, unlike others, where the factual evidence would be necessary to support the defence. Until such factual evidence has been given, there is no basis for the admission of the opinion evidence. The decision not to adduce

33 *Id.* at 23.

the factual evidence at the trial, no doubt because it either was not available or would not have been credible, would have meant that the opinion evidence could not be adduced. Further opinion evidence now tendered relies upon factual statements which are still not supported by any admissible evidence.

As regards the question of credibility, no question of the credibility of Dr. Jones and Professor Bluglass arises, but there are fundamental question whether the statements upon which they have proceeded are worthy of any credit at all. Since those statements are not tendered in any admissible form, it is no necessary to go beyond that. But it is clear that, if a defence of diminished responsibility was to be run, a critical issue would be the creditworthiness of the appellant herself and it is clear beyond doubt that she is not a person who could be treated as a credible witness in matters which affect her own interests in the present matter.

It will accordingly be appreciated that the evidence the subject matter of the appellant's application under section 23 does not afford any ground for allowing her appeal. If received it would do nothing to show that the convictions were unsafe. We repeat, diminished responsibility is exceptional in that it raises an issue upon which the defence has the burden of proof. The appellant has had the opportunity to deploy before the Court admissible fresh evidence which would make such a defence arguable and give a prospect of it being accepted by a jury. She has not placed such evidence before the Court and it follows that there is no basis for treating the jury's verdicts as unsafe. By a parity of reasoning she has failed to persuade us that it is necessary or expedient in the interests if justice to admit any further evidence. We have not applied the dictum of Fenton Atkinson L.J. in *Dodd*, repeated in *Melville*, that the case for diminished responsibility must be 'really overwhelming' before an appellant can be allowed to raise it for the first time in the Court of Appeal. Had we come to the conclusion that the convictions were unsafe, we would have allowed the appeal; that is what the 1995 Act requires.[34]

---

[34] *Id.* at 48.

This judgment contains an authoritative consideration of the Appeal Court's role under Section 23 and Section 2.[35]

This decision may be contrasted with the case of *R. v. Hobson* (1998), which related to an appellant who had stabbed her abusive and alcoholic partner to death during an argument. At the trial she contended that she had acted in self-defense, and there was a subsidiary issue on provocation. She was convicted in 1992. On her appeal heard in 1997, application was made for reception of the evidence of two psychiatrists. They opined that the appellant had been a victim of battered women's syndrome, a condition not recognized in the standard British classification of mental diseases until 1994, and therefore (it was suggested) a condition not considered by British psychiatrists at the date of the trial as capable of founding a plea of diminished responsibility. The Crown resisted the reception of this evidence, relying on a report prepared for the appellant before the trial, which excluded the possibility of a diminished responsibility defense. However, the Court of Appeal ruled that the evidence should be received, and in the light of that decision, the Crown did not seek to support the conviction as safe. A retrial was ordered.[36]

In the 1998 case of *R. v. Shah*, the Court of Appeal summarized the existing case law in the United Kingdom as to retrials due to new defenses and arguments as follows:

> So the decision in each of the cases relied upon turned on the particular facts of that case, and each case emphasises the point that only in wholly exceptional circumstances will this court receive fresh evidence to enable a defence to be advanced which was not put forward at the trial.[37]

In that case, the Appeals judges added that:

> Leaving aside for the moment the one trial principle to which we have referred there are, as it seems to us, other reasons why in this case we should hesitate to exercise our discretion in favour of admitting the fresh evidence. The appellant's own evidence is, as we have said, not capable of belief. The medical evidence

---

35 *See* the *Pearson* judgment, *supra* note 12, paras. 29–31.

36 *See* R. v. Hobson, I Crim. App. R. 31 (1998).

37 R. v. Shah, CACD, Apr. 30, 1998, unreported.

> on which she seeks to rely came into existence long after the relevant time, it initially relied heavily on her account which we have found to be flawed, and it is at variance with the evidence of the other psychiatrists who have been involved in the case. That factor is not, of course, decisive but compare, for example, *Binning* 12th April 1996 unreported, where the fresh evidence was unchallenged. We recognise, of course, that in section 23(2)(b) the word used is "may" but we cannot treat this as a case in which, had the evidence now sought to be relied upon been deployed at trial, the defence of diminished responsibility would have been bound to succeed.[38]

In conclusion, it can be said that the above examples and authorities derived from the U.K. system show that the Court of Appeal follows a case-by-case approach to determine whether new defenses and arguments may justify a retrial. This policy is clearly formulated by the Lord Chief Justice in the *Pearson* case of May 18, 1999:

> From that lengthy recital of authority, it is plain that all applications to adduce fresh evidence under section 23 turn on their own peculiar facts. This is as it should be, since the exercise of a discretionary power must be conditioned by the merits of the case before the Court as the Court perceives them. Since no two cases reaching the Court of Appeal are the same, it will often be hard, if not impossible, to predict with confidence how a Court of Appeal will perceive the merits of any given application in a borderline case, a point which obviously bears on the discharge of the Commission's task under section 13 of the 1995 Act. Judicial reactions, being human, are not uniform. Wisely and correctly, the courts have recognised that the statutory discretion conferred by section 23 cannot be constrained by inflexible mechanistic rules. But the cases do identify certain features which are likely to weigh more or less heavily against the reception of fresh evidence: for example, a deliberate decision by a defendant whose decision-making faculties are unimpaired not to advance before the trial jury a defence known to be available; evidence of mental abnormality or substantial impairment given

38 *Id.*, cited also in *Pearson* judgment, *supra* note 12, paras. 40–41.

> years after the offence and contradicted by evidence available at the time of the offence; expert evidence based on factual premises which are unsubstantiated, unreliable or false, or which is for any other reason unpersuasive. But even features such as these need not be conclusive objections in every case. The overriding discretion conferred on the Court enables it to ensure that, in the last resort, defendants are sentenced for the crimes they have committed and not for psychological failings to which they may be subject.[39]

This paragraph enumerates factors that are relevant to law practice when a new defense or argument may be admitted for retrial. These factors could be applied to other criminal law systems, as well as in the context of international criminal cases.

---

[39] *Pearson* judgment, *supra* note 12, para. 43.

CHAPTER 8

FORENSIC SCIENCES TO PROTECT AGAINST AND REMEDY MISCARRIAGES OF JUSTICE

A. INTRODUCTION: THE EVOLUTION OF FORENSIC GENETICS IN CRIMINAL CASES

Forensic science is a specialization that assists the judiciary and juries in fact-finding and especially in deciding upon guilt or innocence in criminal cases. It draws on a wide range of disciplines, such as biology, chemistry, physics, and mathematics, as well as on more crime-related fields, such as ballistics, fingerprint analysis, tire-prints, sound analysis, and handwriting analysis.[1] Forensic science has proven to be revolutionary in assisting criminal trials, particularly the biological tool of DNA analysis. DNA analysis has become an indispensable and routine part of modern forensic casework, employing extremely sensitive polymerase chain reaction (PCR) techniques to analyze biological material.[2] Accuseds can be definitively linked to crime scenes, or one crime scene to another, using DNA evidence from as little as the saliva on a cigarette butt, skin cells on a steering wheel, or pet hairs on clothing. Large DNA databases can be rapidly scanned for matches to DNA profiles found at the scene of a crime or even partial matches to close relatives of a perpetrator. Unsolved "cold" cases involving sexual assault can be concluded decades after investigations were begun by analyzing degraded DNA from stored swabs or microscope slides.[3] Conversely, DNA analysis techniques can serve as powerful instruments to redress real or potential miscarriages of justice, in that retrials can be sought on the basis of the availability of DNA analysis.

---

1 *See* Mark A. Jobling & Peter Gill, *Encoded Evidence: DNA in Forensic Analysis*, 5 NATURE REVIEWS GENETICS 739 (2004).

2 *Id.*

3 *Id.*

This chapter concentrates on the uses of forensic sciences in general, and especially forensic genetics, for protection against miscarriages of justice, as well as redressing them. This chapter will also ask what the future holds for forensic genetics in this regard, especially in view of new technological developments. The term "forensic genetics" is meant to express the application of genetics to assist the fact-finding process in criminal cases.

B. THE ADVENT OF FORENSIC GENETICS IN THE CONTEXT OF REOPENING INTERNATIONAL CRIMINAL CASES

1. Increasing DNA Exonerations

The last two decades have shown a remarkable development in the growth of forensic genetics as a reliable means of individual identification, with a major impact on international criminal justice systems.[4] Several examples from U.S. law practice have been described in Chapter 5 relating to false confessions that were revealed by DNA evidence. As Jobling and Gill observe: "The increase in sensitivity of DNA methods has allowed the reopening and solving of 'cold' cases and has also led to the exoneration of prisoners (some of whom were awaiting execution convicted through miscarriages of justice)."[5] As to the latter observation, attention should be drawn to the fact that, based on this forensic genetics impact, by October 2000, 82 convicts had been exonerated in North America, 76 in the United States and six in Canada.[6] Interestingly, in 1996 the U.S. Department of Justice issued a report in which post-conviction exonerations were evaluated as of June 1996.[7] This report concluded that, since the advent of forensic DNA testing in 1989, 28 exonerations had occurred by 1996. As a result, as Scheck and Neufeld note, the rate of exonerations in the United States has increased impres-

---

4 *Id.* at 744.

5 *Id.*

6 *See* Barry Scheck & Peter Neufeld, *DNA and Innocence Scholarship*, *in* WRONGLY CONVICTED: PERSPECTIVES ON FAILED JUSTICE 241 (Saundra D. Westervelt & John A. Humphrey eds., 2001).

7 *See* EDWARD CONNORS, THOMAS LUNDREGAN, NEAL MILLER & TOM MCEWAN, CONVICTED BY JURIES, EXONERATED BY SCIENCE: CASE STUDIES IN THE USE OF DNA EVIDENCE TO ESTABLISH INNOCENCE AFTER TRIAL (1996).

sively in the period 1996–2000: 54 in this period versus 28 in the period 1989–1996.[8] Reflecting on these figures, these authors remark that "the significance of the DNA exonerations does not lie simply in the extraordinary number of documented miscarriages of justice but in the unique certainty of the innocence determinations and the concomitant utility such certainty brings to revealing and studying the strengths and weaknesses of the criminal justice system."[9] Thus, the question is: what are, or should be, precise implications, for future protection against miscarriages of justice in both national and international criminal cases? To come to a proper answer to this fundamental question, it is important to first arrive at an understanding of new and contemporary DNA technology.

2. Technical Evolution of Forensic Genetics

When one overviews the development of forensic genetic technology from its inception in 1989, three stages may be detected. The first generation or category of forensic DNA tests was based upon the use of the "restriction fragment length polymorphism" (RFLP) technique. This method was characterized as having strong and weak elements. Its strong element related to its power of discrimination. Based on a valid RFLP match at a number of DNA markers on a definitive part of biological evidence, such as on a vaginal swab in a rape case relating to one suspect, there is a considerable possibility that an innocent person can be exonerated or a guilty person incriminated.[10] However, RFLP testing was not very sensitive in that it required a comparatively large amount of high-molecular-weight DNA in a crime scene sample to have a reliable result.[11]

The second generation and category of forensic DNA testing was introduced as the "DQ alpha polymarker test" and was based on the polymerase chain reaction (PCR) method, which was developed in 1988. This method has been characterized as "molecular xeroxing."[12] DNA

---

8 Scheck & Neufeld, *supra* note 6, at 241.

9 *Id.*

10 *Id.* at 242.

11 *Id.*

12 *Id.*

amplification by PCR provides an enormous increase in sensitivity, allowing minute amounts of degraded DNA to be analyzed. PCR-based methods now form the basis of all forensic DNA typing.[13] Importantly, very little DNA is required to analyze, through PCR, the DQ alpha polymarker DNA markers.[14] Even based upon "small or old, degraded samples" extremely sensitive results have been obtained with the DQ alpha polymarker test, and exonerations of accuseds have been established even after an RFLP test of insufficient DNA had failed to get a result.[15] Yet the discriminating potential of DQ alpha testing is limited when it concerns mixed samples (i.e., samples from two or more persons of a blood, saliva, or semen stain). The discovery of the so-called "short tandem repeats" (STRs) led to an improvement in discriminatory power.[16] In this context, Jobling and Gill remark that "the use of STRs supplanted both the early PCR and SLP tests worldwide once their advantages of high discriminating power, sensitivity and ability to resolve simple mixtures were realized. In addition, the time needed to carry out an analysis was greatly reduced."[17] In fact, STRs constitute a revised or reformed PCR-based forensic DNA test that combines both the discriminating power of RFLP and the sensitivity of DQ alpha testing. This is due to the fact that the STR test involves 13 DNA markers, as well as a marker that sex-types samples. Accordingly, this test has played an important role in exonerating accuseds.[18]

The third generation or category of forensic genetics pertains to mitochondrial DNA testing (mtDNA). According to Scheck and Neufeld, this technique will contribute to exonerating even more wrongfully convicted persons.[19] Unlike STR testing, mtDNA analyzes DNA from a cell's nucleus. MtDNA testing is based on the PCR technique, yet it offers more precision since its "molecular xeroxing" capacity is directed at sequences of mtDNA found in a cell.[20] One of the advantages of mtDNA lies in its copy number, which is between 200 and 1,700 per

---

13 *See* Jobling & Gill, *supra* note 1, at 741.

14 *See* Scheck & Neufeld, *supra* note 6, at 242.

15 *Id.*

16 *See* Jobling & Gill, *supra* note 1, at 741.

17 *Id.*

18 See Scheck & Neufeld, *supra* note 6, at 243.

19 *Id.*

20 *Id.*

cell, meaning that it has a greater probability of survival than nuclear DNA. This makes it capable of analyzing old or severely damaged samples, or samples that are low in DNA, such as hair shafts. In addition, while autosomal or nuclear DNA contains only two copies of each gene, mtDNA, which is spread throughout a cell, is copied many thousands of times. As a result, as mtDNA is much more available in a biological sample than nuclear DNA, mtDNA testing is much more sensitive.[21] In other words, an mtDNA test enables scientists to conduct a DNA test on, for instance, a hair without a nucleus. That is to say, mtDNA can be extracted from the shaft of a rootless hair. As a result, miscarriages of justices may be revealed when previous inferior microscopic research on hairs have failed to exonerate an accused.

As an example of the value of mtDNA as a potential mechanism to redress miscarriages of justice, consider the "Central Park Jogger" case of December 2002, in which five men were exonerated due to mtDNA analysis:

> On the night of April 19, 1989, a 28-year-old jogger was brutally attacked and raped in Central Park. She was found unconscious with her skull fractured, her body temperature at 84 degrees, and 75 percent of her blood drained from her body. When she recovered, she had no memory of the assault. Initial police investigations quickly focused on a group of African, American and Latino youths who were in police custody for a series of other attacks perpetrated in the park that night. After prolonged periods of police interrogation, five teenagers—Yusef Salaam, Kevin Richardson, Antron McCray, Raymond Santana and Kharey Wise—confessed to being involved in the attacks. At the time, the defendants were between 14 and 16 years of age. Richardson, McCray, Santana, and Wise all gave videotaped confessions. The confessions were presented as evidence, though they differed as to the time, location, and participants of the rape. At trial, the prosecutors also presented forensic evidence, including hair found on one of the defendants that "matched and resembled" that of the victim and a hair found on the victim's clothing that was believed to have originated from one of the defendants.

---

[21] *Id.*

> Also presented as evidence was a rock found near the scene of the crime that had blood and hair on it; evidence that was believed to have come from the victim. . . . All five teenagers were convicted, in two separate trials, of charges stemming from the attack. . . . In early 2002, Matias Reyes, a convicted murderer and rapist, admitted that he alone was responsible for the attack on the Central Park jogger. Reyes had already committed another rape near Central Park days earlier in 1989, using the same *modus operandi*. The victim of that rape described the rapist as having fresh stitches in his chin and an investigator quickly linked Reyes to this description. Although the police had Reyes's name on file, they failed to connect Reyes to the rape and assault of the Central Park jogger. . . . Eventually, the evidence from the crime was subjected to DNA testing. The DNA profile obtained from the spermatozoa found in the rape kit matched the profile of Reyes. Mitochondrial DNA testing on the hairs found on one of the defendants revealed that the hairs were not related to the victim or the crime. The evidence corroborates Reyes's confession to the crime and is consistent with the other crimes committed by Reyes. He is currently serving a life sentence for those crimes. . . . On December 19, 2002, on the recommendation of the Manhattan District Attorney, the convictions of the five men were overturned.[22]

Yet, mtDNA testing has its evidentiary and forensic scientific limitations, which pertain to its comparative lack of discriminatory power. Scheck and Neufeld describe this disadvantage as follows: "Mitochondrial DNA is inherited maternally. Unless something strange is occurring within a family, brothers and sisters and maternal cousins will have the same mitochondrial pattern as each other and their mothers; they should not match their fathers! Thus, mitochondrial testing has limited value in distinguishing among family members and statistically is not as powerful as STR or RFLP testing. Nonetheless, it is a useful tool in some old and new cases."[23]

The fourth generation of developing DNA techniques relates to the low copy number (LCN) method, advanced in 2001. This method is based

---

22 *See* www.innocenceproject.org/case/display_profile.php?id=119.

23 *See* Scheck & Neufeld, *supra* note 6, at 244.

on an increase of PCR amplification cycles. "By increasing the number of PCR amplification cycles, it was demonstrated that the technique could be utilised to amplify <100 pg of total genomic DNA. These levels of DNA have been termed low copy number (LCN). The increase in sensitivity of the amplification reaction facilitates the examination of a whole new range of evidence types that were previously not possible because of the very low amounts of DNA present in the sample."[24] The relevance of the LCN method to the protection against miscarriages of justice are the following:

(1) Hyperamplification of LCN DNA samples has proven to be an efficient and reliable method when DNA profiles have to be generated from samples that contain minute amounts of genomic DNA.[25]

(2) The forensic scientists Kloosterman and Kersbergen observe that:

> Amplification of DNA under LCN conditions holds promising new applications in the forensic context. One foreseeable application is the typing of a small numbers of haploid sperm cells or diploid cells that have been separated out of suspended cells from mixed cell stains by the use of flow cytometry. This approach will ease the often cumbersome and labour-intensive interpretation of profiles from mixtures. The LCN typing system has proved its merit in DNA identification of decomposed human remains. We have shown that reliable typing results were obtained from 10-year-old bones. Until now, mtDNA typing was considered to be the most sensitive system and the only possibility when the authorities demand the DNA identification of old bone samples. Due to the higher speed of analysis and the unsurpassed evidential value that is obtained through multiplex STR typing it can be

---

[24] J.P. Whitaker, E.A. Cotton & P. Gill, *A Comparison of the Characteristics of Profiles Produced with the AMPF1STR(r) SGM PlusTM Multiplex System for Both Standard and Low Copy Number (LCN) STR DNA Analysis*, 123 FORENSIC SCI. INT'L 215 (2001).

[25] *See* Ate D. Kloosterman & Paula Kersbergen, *Efficacy and Limits of Genotyping Low Copy Number (LCN) DNA Samples by Multiplex PCR of STR Loci*, unpublished.

foreseen that LCN typing systems will supersede mtDNA typing and improve the identification of skeletal remains.[26]

(3) This new LCN method, in order to serve as a forensic mechanism to protect against or redress miscarriages of justice,

> requires a completely different approach when samples are collected from exhibits, scenes of crime or *corpora delicti*. Due to the diversity of evidential samples that have the potential to contain minute amounts of DNA evidence from which a profile can be generated, the forensic scientist and other scene-of-crime personnel must have a clear understanding of the unprecedented possibilities of this new technology. The strategy of the investigators at the crime scene must amalgamate with the new possibilities of LCN profiling. Furthermore, the application of the LCN DNA technology can be of major importance when the authorities demand the review and reinvestigation of unsolved crime cases from the past.[27]

3. Practical Problems and Complications of Assessing the Evidentiary Weight of DNA Evidence

Miscarriages of justices in criminal cases can be prevented or redressed when judges, prosecutors, and defense counsel, guided by the technical insight contained in the preceding section, adduce the proper evidentiary weight to DNA evidence. Two practical problems and complications should be explained:

First, the British scientists Jobling and Gill offer this illustrative example of the dangers of false interpretation of DNA test results:

> The evidential weight of a match between crime stain profile and suspect is quantified by the match probability (*Pm*); the chance of two unrelated people sharing a profile. For independently inherited loci, *Pm* is calculated by multiplying the

---

26 *Id.*

27 *Id.*

individual allele frequencies in the profile in question (the "product rule"): the greater the number of loci, and the greater the heterozygosity of each locus, the lower the value of *Pm*. However, there are a number of situations in which *Pm* can be substantially increased:

- if the profile is partial because of degradation, reducing the number of informative loci;
- if a suspect and a perpetrator share many alleles by descent (for example, are brothers);
- if a suspect and a perpetrator originate from the same subpopulation.

Population structure can cause frequencies of alleles (and hence profiles) to vary between subpopulations—an issue that caused great controversy in the application of SLP profiling. The debate was resolved by applying guidelines to ensure match probabilities quoted in court were conservative (that is, favourable to the defendant). Similar conservatism is now applied to STR profiles.

Despite the high discriminating power of very low *Pm* values, interpretation in the courtroom has not been without controversy, and this is because of the way that DNA evidence is sometimes presented. A well-known example is the "prosecutor's fallacy," or "fallacy of the transposed conditional": suppose a crime is committed in London (population ~ 7 million) and a crime-scene profile is obtained that has a 10^{-6}. The prosecutor, finding that a defendant matches the profile, might say: "The odds are a million to one in favour of the defendant being guilty." But, given the population size, ~7 people in the city are expected to match the profile, so it can then be argued that the odds are actually 7 to 1 in favour of innocence; however, this "defence fallacy" unrealistically assumes that each of the 7 people has equal probability of guilt, which is untrue as DNA evidence is not used in isolation. This problem of logic can be avoided by an approach based on a likelihood ratio, using conditional probabilities based on prosecution and defence scenarios: the job of

> the court, based on an evaluation of both DNA and non-DNA evidence, is to decide the ultimate issue of guilt or innocence, given *all* of the evidence. Under complex scenarios with many different variables, "Bayesian networks"—intuitive graphical means to display hypotheses regarding the probabilistic relationships between variables—are a powerful aid to understanding, although they are not intended to supplant the role of the jury.[28]

Second, the same British experts point to various interpretative dangers that are of relevance to the criminal law practice. In an overview, they enumerate several of those factors:

> Several factors can complicate the interpretation of DNA profiles. These include mixed samples and the availability of only small amounts of DNA, which (in the UK) is analysed by "low-copy number" (LCN) methods and can lead to allele drop-out. LCN analysis also increases the probability of contamination (additional "foreign" alleles in the profile), despite stringent precautions to prevent it. Contamination can be gross and lead to full additional profiles, where typically the negative control will be affected; these can be searched against forensic staff elimination databases and stored in a separate database to allow detection and monitoring of problems such as contamination of plasticware during manufacture. Alternatively, contamination can contribute an extra one or two alleles per DNA profile (allele drop-in), where the negative control is usually unaffected. The probabilities of a match, of drop-out and of contamination (based on computer simulation analysis of negative control data) can be readily incorporated into the calculation of the likelihood ratio (LR) when the significance of the DNA evidence is being assessed; calculations are complex but are aided by a computer program (LoComatioN) that can also combine the results of several profiles into a single LR. Here, we no longer think of a DNA profile either matching or not matching a suspect, because the twin effects of drop-in and drop-out will alter the suspect's apparent profile so that it does not match the crime scene sample, without indicating an exclusion; rather, the probability of the

28 Jobling & Gill, *supra* note 1, at 742.

evidence is lowered. Anomalous profiles can arise from causes other than mixtures but can readily be resolved by careful analysis:

- Mutations in the PCR primer target region can cause allele drop-out or heterozygote imbalance.
- An STR can be duplicated and segregated in a normal Mendelian fashion or a somatic STR mutation occurring early in development can lead to a three-peak profile for the STR, which might vary between tissues, examples are on STR Base. . . .
- The STR D21S11 can reveal three alleles in trisomy 21 cases. . . .
- Discordant results in the amelogenin sex test can be observed in rare individuals, including cases of sex-reversal (XX males and XY females) and males carrying deletions that remove AMELY.
- A true mixed profile can also originate from a single individual. Analysis of DNA from people who had undergone successful bone marrow transplants > 5 years previously, showed a mixed profile in buccal and fingernail samples; in blood, the recipient's own profile had been completely replaced by that of the donor, whereas in hair, the recipient's profile remained unmixed.[29]

The above-mentioned two factors and examples should make the judiciary, prosecution, and advocacy mindful to the evidentiary relativity of DNA evidence in criminal cases. Without such consciousness, the danger for rendering wrongful convictions is more prominent.

4. Future Forensic Genetics Developments and Miscarriages of Justice

The above discussions showed that forensic genetics have played an important role in protection against miscarriages of justice and will continue to serve this purpose. Increasing technical developments in DNA

29 *Id.* at 744.

testing will be instrumental in this role. It is important that law practitioners increasingly familiarize themselves with these developments in order to contribute to this development. After all, it is not the forensic expert who rules upon guilt or innocence.[30]

As to the future of forensic genetics, two major likelihoods lie ahead. First, molecular biological approaches to the identification of blood, semen, and saliva stains using analysis of specific mRNAs[31] (which are surprisingly stable) have been described and will probably increase in use and importance.[32] Second, as our understanding of the genetic basis of disease and differences in the response to drugs increases, forensic genetics will be increasingly applied to determining the cause of death—"forensic molecular pathology."[33]

C. FORENSIC EVIDENCE STANDARDS TO PREVENT MISCARRIAGES OF JUSTICE IN CRIMINAL TRIALS

1. Introduction

Contemporary criminal cases have shown that forensic sciences, and particularly advanced DNA testing, may prevent and redress miscarriages of justice.[34] At the same time, failure to properly apply and admit forensic techniques and standards in criminal cases can be a cause for wrongful convictions. This section looks into these factors, while at the same time assessing forensic evidence standards that can assist domestic and international criminal trial judges in evaluating criminal evidence.

---

30 *See* Chapter 9 for this restriction.

31 Messenger or mRNA is a copy of the information carried by a gene on the DNA. *See* http://www.biochem.uwo.ca/meds/medna/mRNA.html.

32 *See* Jobling & Gill, *supra* note 1, at 749.

33 *Id.*

34 *See also* the examples described in Chapter 5.

2. Forensic Science Errors in the Diagnosis of Guilt or Innocence in Criminal Cases

a. The Reality of Contemporary Forensic Science Errors

Notwithstanding the important value of forensic science within the fact-finding process, which underlies every criminal procedure, the reality is that the history of wrongful convictions in the United States and the United Kingdom has been paralleled by erroneous and even sometimes fraudulent forensic science.[35]

Research in the United States into contemporary forensic science errors reveals, in addition to crime lab fraud, inadvertent error, sloppiness, exaggeration, and bias as factors of forensic science error.[36] These errors are particularly evident in the area of "cross-contamination of evidence," i.e., the resulting impact of one piece of evidence on another. Castelle and Loftus describe this pertinent mechanism as follows:

> In the forensic sciences, for example, certain types of testing can produce ambiguous results that may be interpreted using a high degree of subjective judgment. Consider a forensic scientist faced with ambiguous test results who has been informed that the suspect was identified by the victim. Because he or she may be affected by that knowledge, even unwittingly, the scientist may read into those results a confirmation of guilt that might not otherwise be apparent (Thompson 1997). The less neutral the scientist or the more the scientist feels a part of the prosecution team, the more likely that non-scientific evidence will bias the supposedly neutral scientific results. The most extreme examples, of course, are the *Zain* cases, in which Zain, as a state trooper and a forensic scientist, appears to have deter-

---

[35] *See* George Castelle & Elizabeth F. Loftus, *Misinformation and Wrongful Convictions*, *in* WRONGLY CONVICTED: PERSPECTIVES ON FAILED JUSTICE 28 (Saundra D. Westervelt & John A. Humphrey eds., 2001), which authors describe several U.S. cases in support of this observation, especially the *William Harris* case. William Harris was exonerated by DNA testing in 1993 after being convicted of sexual assault and sentenced to ten to 20 years in a West Virginia penitentiary.

[36] *Id.* at 28–29, referring to a 1999 study by George Castelle of 1999 on the "lessons learned" from the *William Harris* case.

> mined first who was the principal police suspect and then simply produced whatever combination of real and fictional scientific data served to confirm guilt.[37]

From this it may be seen that two factors may intensify cross-contamination of evidence: scientific evidence may have a considerable influence and weight on the testimony of lay witnesses, and evidence from lay witnesses is capable of influencing scientific results.[38] As to the first element, the *William Harris* case in the United States provides an illustrative example of this contaminating effect; the scientist's "knowledge" that scientific testing had confirmed her identification of Harris strengthened her confidence that she was right.[39]

Within the context of retrial proceedings, due attention should thus be paid to the issue of the cross-contaminating effect of misinformation. A thorough understanding of the potential for cross-contamination of forensic evidence is therefore of perennial concern in preventing and redressing miscarriages of justice.[40]

b. 11 Factors

Before discussing forensic sciences standards, it is relevant to point to 11 forensic errors which could lead to wrongful convictions:

(1) overstating the strength of results;

(2) overstating the frequency of genetic matches on individual pieces of evidence;

(3) misreporting the frequency of genetic matches on multiple pieces of evidence;

(4) reporting that multiple items of evidence had been tested, when only a single item had been tested;

(5) reporting inconclusive results as conclusive;

---

37 *Id.* at 29–30.

38 *Id.* at 30.

39 *Id.*

40 *Id.* at 31.

(6) repeatedly altering laboratory records;

(7) grouping results to create the erroneous impression that genetic markers had been obtained from all samples tested;

(8) failing to report conflicting results;

(9) failing to conduct or to report conducting additional testing to resolve conflicting results;

(10) implying a match with a suspect when testing supported only a match with the victim; and

(11) reporting scientifically impossible or improbable results.[41]

It is thus important to make a distinction between the scientific techniques and the validity of the underlying theory, when it concerns the assessment of forensic evidentiary issues within international criminal law. In this connection, two guidelines are important.

First, the acceptance of a particular DNA technique or report of a forensic pathologist does not say anything about the theory or hypothesis that underlies the particular technique. This means that criminal courts can, while accepting the method, still reject the interpretation of the forensic materials. In addition, the interpretation of the forensic test results can be disputed and be moot, despite the validity of the underlying forensic science technique (for instance, the application of the LCN method in DNA cases).[42]

Second, it should be stressed that "as powerful as DNA analysis is, it is far from being the *sine qua non* of forensic casework. DNA evidence must always be considered within the framework of other evidence of many types, and the role of the forensic geneticist is not to make presumptions of guilt or innocence, but to provide unbiased information to judge and jury."[43] The latter observation may already prevent wrongful convictions due to an overstretching of the impact of DNA results in criminal cases.

---

41 These elements are derived from a U.S. Report in Re Investigation of the West Virginia State Police Crime Lab, Serology Division, 438 S.E.2d 501, 503 (1993).

42 *See* for this technique Section B.2 of this chapter.

43 *See* Jobling & Gill, *supra* note 1, at 739.

c. *Forensic Science Errors: The* Brandon Mayfield *Case*

The most problematic aspect of forensic science lies not in its potential scientific validity, but in its diagnostic value as to the determination of guilt or innocence in international criminal cases. The determination of what constitutes evidence capable of supporting a conviction under international criminal law should take account of not only the above-mentioned forensic errors, but also the fact that forensic science is not meant to substitute a tribunal of fact in that it may assume a judgment on guilt or innocence in criminal cases. This view is reinforced by the *Brandon Mayfield* case, in which the U.S. Federal Bureau of Investigation (FBI) on May 25, 2004, mistakenly linked a fingerprint of American lawyer Brandon Mayfield (a 37-year-old convert to Islam) to one found near the scene of the terrorist bombing in Madrid (Spain) on March 11, 2004, which killed 190 people and injured almost 2,000 others. This forensic error led to the false imprisonment of Mayfield for two weeks, and ended only after the dismissal of the criminal case against him by a U.S. district judge on May 25, 2004. A central point in this false accusation was the role and functioning of forensic science, particularly the diagnostic value of forensic science as to the determination of criminal guilt or innocence. The origin of the false arrest sprang from an error by the FBI's supercomputer for matching fingerprints, which was first analyzed by the FBI's own experts.[44] The case against Mayfield started when FBI fingerprint analysts in Quantico, Virginia, searched for possible matches to a digital image of a fingerprint found on a bag of detonators the day of the Spanish bombings on March 11. The FBI fingerprint system returned 15 possible matches, including prints belonging to Mayfield, on file from a 1984 burglary arrest in Wichita, Kansas, when Mayfield was a teenager. Three separate FBI examiners narrowed the identification to Mayfield, according to FBI agent Robert Jordan. Notably, a court-appointed fingerprint expert agreed with this analysis. The FBI maintained its certainty even as Spanish authorities said by mid-April that the original image of the fingerprint taken directly from the bag did not match Mayfield's. In the beginning of May 2004, Spanish authorities informed the United States that the fingerprints of an Algerian man were on the bag. According to Jordan, FBI examiners flew to Spain,

---

44 For this case, *see* http://www.msnbc.msn.com/id/503007.

viewed the original print pattern of the fingerprint on paper, and agreed that it was not Mayfield's.

As additional evidence in support of Mayfield's arrest, the FBI had relied on Mayfield's attendance at a local mosque, his advertising legal services in a publication owned by a man suspected to have links to terrorism, and a telephone call his wife placed to a branch of an Islamic charity with suspected terrorist ties. The FBI also noted that Mayfield represented a man in a child custody case who later pleaded guilty to conspiring to help Al Qaeda and the Taliban fight U.S. forces in Afghanistan. According to the case file, FBI agents began their surveillance of Mayfield two weeks after the attacks in the Spanish capital. Under a provision of the U.S. Patriot Act, they entered his home without his knowledge, but aroused the family's suspicion by bolting the wrong lock on their way out and leaving a footprint on the rug that did not match any family members.

The potential vulnerability of the invocation of forensic sciences in support of a determination of guilt or innocence in criminal cases is reflected by what happened afterwards in the *Mayfield* case. In a study conducted by Professor Itiel Dror of the University of Southampton, five professional forensic examiners were each presented with two sets of prints, one purportedly from Mr. Mayfield and the other from the Madrid bombings. The research question for these five examiners was whether they could assess what the FBI examiners in the *Mayfield* case had done wrong. One examiner said that he could not tell if the pair matched, while three other examiners concluded that the pair did not match. The fifth examiner insisted that the prints did match. What the examiners were not aware of, however, was that the set of prints were neither from Madrid nor from Mr. Mayfield. These pairs of fingerprints were, in fact, pairs that each of these five examiners had testified in recent criminal cases came from the same person. The three examiners who told the scientists that the pair did not match, therefore, reached a conclusion opposite to the one they had given formerly in court; another examiner now expressed uncertainty, whereas in court he had been certain.[45] This study shows that, with respect to traditional forensic sciences analysis of bite marks, bullets, hair, handwriting, and fingerprints, a serious critical

---

[45] For this experiment *see* The WALL ST. J. EUROPE (Technology, Management, Marketing) SCI. J., Oct. 7–9, 2005, at A11.

approach is required to reassert the scientific value attributed to these methods in the past.

Therefore, the incentive for assessing guilt or innocence in criminal cases on the basis of forensic sciences, however important this may be when assisting the jury or a trier of fact in understanding the evidence before it, should be nuanced in that the role of forensic sciences in international criminal cases is not misconceived: it is merely in place to assist the judge or jury in understanding the evidence, rather than leading the judge or jury into a determination of criminal guilt.[46]

D. SCIENTIFIC ERROR: A POTENTIAL RETRIAL ARGUMENT

Forensic science is not a perfect science; it cannot determine guilt or innocence in criminal cases with mathematical precision. The Australian forensic scientist, Ian Freckleton, cautions against an over-estimate of the value of forensic sciences in criminal cases, saying that "scientific error has been revealed as contributing to a worrying degree to the incidence of miscarriages of justice over the past 20 years in the United States, the United Kingdom and Australia."[47] Miscarriages of justice by reason of flawed forensic science can even occur in the context of "honest science and testimony."[48] Two mechanisms may be used in order to prevent or redress these types of miscarriages: the establishment of a "sound system of supervision, review and peer assessment of (forensic sciences) results to ensure both capacity for replication and validity;"[49] and extension of grounds for retrial in international criminal cases, in that a retrial could be allowed when new forensic evidence proves the inaccuracy of the scientific materials that underlie the conviction. This goes particularly for those criminal convictions that are solely (or to a decisive extent) based on such materials. This suggested extension of retrial possibilities, based on the phenomenon of "error in science," seems also warranted in view of the dangers of "biased" forensic science evidence. Even forensic science is not immune to the mech-

---

46 For this role of forensic experts, *see* Section F; *see also* Chapters 9 and 10.

47 *See* Ian Freckleton, *A Taxonomy of Error and Deviance, in* HARMONISATION IN FORENSIC EXPERTISE 319–20 (J.F. Nijboer & W.J.J.M. Sprangers eds., 2000).

48 *Id.*

49 *Id.* at 335, 336–37.

anism that "expectation can lead to self-deception and self-deception to the potential to believe too readily, to be deceived."[50] Freckleton explains the cause of this mechanism, saying that "one of the difficulties that accompanies the fact that forensic scientists working in state-funded laboratories do work exclusively or most exclusively for police clients is that the task set for them by their clients is consistently to advise whether, as the investigators anticipate, samples will match. There is an investigative expectation that they will."[51]

An example of such a forensic "self-fulfilling prophecy" can be seen in the Dutch landmark case of *Prosecutor v. Viets/Dubois* (the Puttense homicide case), which led to a retrial ordered by the Dutch Supreme Court on June 26, 2001,[52] and ultimately to an acquittal of the two defendants on April 24, 2002, rendered by a Court of Appeal (Leeuwarden) in the Netherlands.[53] The evidence disclosed during the retrial in this case revealed a high degree of "investigative expectation" on the part of the police, which affected the forensic researchers' starting point. In this regard, the British case of *R. v. Deen* should also be of guidance when assessing this retrial argument. In *R. v. Deen* the Court of Appeal held that one should be mindful of the dangers of "investigative expectations" in criminal cases, "warning scientists not to fall into the trap of the prosecutor's fallacy, namely confusing the match probability that an innocent person would match the NCA sample from the crime scene, a matter upon which they are entitled to act as experts, with the likelihood ratio, which is the probability that the matching individual before the Court is innocent, a matter for the jury."[54] When one accepts that forensic scientists, under circumstances, are falsely led to a causal connection between their own hypothesis and the conclusion of the particular investigation, one should also acknowledge the observation that "he or she has a tendency to commit errors of interpretation in favour of the expectation."[55]

---

50 *Id.* at 326.

51 *Id.*

52 *See* Dutch Jurisprudence (NJ) 2001, 564.

53 The two defendants were initially convicted to ten years imprisonment for manslaughter and rape; for this case, *see* G.G.J. Knoops, *De Puttense Moordzaak*, *in* 29 NEDERLANDS JURISTENBLAD 1402–07 (2002).

54 *See* R. v. Deen, judgment, Jan. 10, 1994.

55 *See* Freckleton, *supra* note 47, at 327.

Another illustrative example of the danger to perceive forensic science as an absolute judicial mechanism, to ascertain guilt or innocence in criminal cases, forms another Dutch landmark case in the area of miscarriages of justice, namely that of *Prosecutor v. Louwes*. On September, 25 1999, Mrs. Wittenberg was found dead at her residence in Deventer (the Netherlands). From the forensic post-mortem analysis of the corpse, the police concluded that Mrs. Wittenberg had been killed by strangulation and/or stabbings with a sharp object, causing five stab wounds in her chest. The police assumed immediately that there had been only one perpetrator, an assumption, however, that has never been forensically established as being correct. In the victim's residence, no traces of damage caused by forced entry were found. From this observation, the police (and at a later stage, also the courts) concluded that the perpetrator and the victim had not been strangers to each other.

Ernest Louwes, who had been the victim's tax consultant for five years, became the only suspect of this crime. On March 9, 2000, the District Court of Zwolle acquitted Louwes of the charges brought against him, and his provisional detention was terminated. After appeal by the prosecutor, the Court of Appeal in Arnhem reversed the decision of the District Court of Zwolle in its judgment of December, 22, 2000, and found Louwes guilty.

The key evidence, on which the decision of the Court of Appeal of Arnhem was based, was related to the alleged murder weapon, a knife found in the vicinity, about 1.5 km away from the crime scene several days after the presumed time of death of the victim. Louwes then appealed to the Dutch Supreme Court. In its decision of November 20, 2001, the Supreme Court dismissed the appeal in cassation, and the conviction thus became final.

In July 2003, the Dutch Supreme Court granted a request to reopen the case based on new DNA research, which led to the observation that, on the particular knife, no DNA material of the victim could be detected, that both the absence of DNA of the victim on the knife and the absence of the requisite unambiguous relationship between the knife and the crime for the probative value of the "scent-identification-test" raised serious doubts as to the evidentiary construction contained in the judgment of the Court of Appeal Arnhem. According to the Dutch Supreme

Court, these observations should reasonably have led to the acquittal of Louwes.

However, on February 9, 2004, the Court of Appeal in Den Bosch upheld the conviction of the Court of Appeal of Arnhem. Remarkably, it did so on totally different evidentiary grounds. Yet, the Court of Appeal of Den Bosch held that the initial conviction rendered by the Court of Appeal Arnhem and the evidentiary construction applied by the latter Court, was incorrect, in particular now that the knife could not be considered the murder weapon. In this case the Supreme Court had concluded in its ruling of July 1, 2005, that an acquittal of Louwes would have been a likely outcome if, at the time, it had been known to the Court of Appeal Arnhem that the knife was not the murder weapon. This conclusion by the Supreme Court was therefore set aside by the Court of Appeal of Den Bosch,[56] when it accepted the prosecution's new evidence. This new evidence consisted of DNA traces, allegedly to be attributed to both the victim and Mr. Louwes, which traces the investigators of the Dutch Forensic Institute only discovered on the blouse of the victim four years and four months after the crime. Notably, the same blouse had already been examined by police and the Dutch Forensic Institute in the period September 1999–December 2003. The late "discovery" of the trace on the blouse, and its alleged traces, were never before introduced in any of the court proceedings. They were only presented for the first time in the revision procedure in the beginning of 2004. The blouse (and its alleged characteristics or properties) was not introduced as a piece of evidence, nor was it an issue of consideration in any of the preceding court proceedings (District Court Zwolle, Court of Appeal Arnhem, Supreme Court in cassation and Supreme Court in reopening procedure). After analyzing the results of the examination of the blouse, the prosecution expert witness concluded that these results allegedly supported the hypothesis that the cell material on the blouse was transmitted during a violent incident.

Before the new physical and biochemical investigations of the blouse were carried out at the end of 2003, it was found wrapped up in an unsealed open paper bag. The bag was put in a box inside a bigger box containing other materials originating from the crime scene and materials belonging to Louwes.

---

56 See Court of 's-Hertogenbosch, judgment, Feb. 9, 2004, para. 2.4.

After closure of the criminal case, the defense requested a second opinion from the British Forensic Sciences Services (FSS) in Birmingham, in that the conclusions of the Dutch Forensic Institute regarding the hypothesis (that the DNA traces did not stem from a businesslike contact but rather from a violent incident) were reviewed. In their report of March 31, 2006, the forensic experts of FSS concluded, *inter alia:*

> Given the inconsistencies surrounding the packaging and storage of the blouse, another possible alternative that has to be considered is: the cell material from Mr. Louwes has been transferred as a result of contamination from other items stained with DNA from Mr. Louwes.

In the second place, the experts of FSS concluded that "the traces of DNA do not constitute direct evidence but that they may have indirect evidential significance as they can indicate that a suspect was present at a scene or has had some form of contact with the victim."

In the third place, the experts of FSS provided another potential explanation for the presence of the DNA on the blouse, namely that cell material from Mr. Louwes was transferred as a result of normal businesslike contacts between him and Mrs. Wittenberg, but was subsequently transferred to the blouse by either the "true offender" or by another individual unrelated to the offense.

Lastly and in essence, the British experts held that they were not able to determine whether the DNA on the blouse was more likely to have been deposited as a result of violent transfer rather than businesslike contact. Following this second opinion, the defense moved again for reopening of the criminal case against Mr. Louwes, purporting that there had been an error in science, while the judges unjustly used the DNA traces as direct and main evidence for the guilt of Mr. Louwes to the murder. The Louwes case illustrates how circumspect judges should interpret DNA materials in criminal cases and that DNA, as such, does not tell us anything about guilt or innocence *per se*.

Henceforth, and by way of conclusion, a retrial in international criminal cases should be available in case of "error in science" as set forth in this section.

E. FORENSIC STANDARDS AND PRINCIPLES TO BE APPLIED BY NATIONAL AND INTERNATIONAL CRIMINAL COURTS: THE APPROACH OF THE U.S. SUPREME COURT

To prevent "error in science" and potential miscarriages of justice, and also to set forth arguments for redressing them, national and international criminal courts should adhere to a set of basic principles derived from U.S. federal law and case law.

Rule 702 of the U.S. *Federal Rules of Evidence* could be of guidance. It states: "If scientific, technical, or other specialized knowledge will assist the trier of fact to understand the evidence or to determine a fact in issue, a witness qualified as an expert by knowledge, skill, experience training or education, may testify thereto in the form of an opinion or otherwise, if (1) the testimony is based upon sufficient facts or data, (2) the testimony is the product of reliable principles and methods, and (3) the witness has applied the principles and methods reliably to the facts of the case."[57]

As to the compliance with this rule, the judgment in *Frye v. United States* is helpful: "Just when a scientific principle or discovery crosses the line between the experimental and demonstrable stages is difficult to define. Somewhere in this twilight zone the evidential force of the principle must be recognized, and while the courts will go a long way in admitting expert testimony deduced from a well recognized scientific principle or discovery, the thing from which the deduction is made must be sufficiently established to have gained general acceptance in the particular field in which it belongs."[58] In other words, the *Frye* test developed in the United States rejects scientific evidence, unless it is of a type that is generally accepted as valid by professional opinion. The *Frye* decision provoked considerable controversy, as it clearly curtailed criminal courts in the use of the latest advances of scientific knowledge.[59]

---

57 *See* U.S. FED. R. EVID., effective on Dec. 1, 2000.

58 *See* Frye v. United States, 293 F. 1013, 1014 (D.C. Cir. 1923); in this case, the rule was used to exclude polygraph (lie-detector) test evidence.

59 *See* John R. Spencer, *Evidence and Forensic Science, in* HARMONISATION IN FORENSIC EXPERTISE 552 (J.F. Nijboer & W.J.J.M. Sprangers eds., 2000).

Predictably, in 1993, the U.S. Supreme Court overturned the *Frye* decision in the case of *Daubert v. Merell Dow Pharmaceutical Inc.*[60] The Supreme Court, in this case, promulgated the test that the expert findings are to be based on "sound science" (see below).

In *Daubert*, the U.S. Supreme Court ruled that the *Frye* test (i.e., saying that expert opinion based on a scientific technique was admissible if it is "generally accepted" as reliable in the relevant scientific community) no longer functions as a standard for the admission of expert testimony. The U.S. Supreme Court articulated its new test on this area as follows:

> Faced with a proffer of expert testimony, then, the trial judge must determine at the outset, pursuant to Rule 104(a), whether the expert is proposing to testify to (1) scientific knowledge that (2) will assist the trier of fact to understand or determine a fact in issue. This entails a preliminary assessment of whether that reasoning or methodology properly can be applied to the facts in issue.[61]

The U.S. Supreme Court defined several factors which have bearing on the question whether a method is scientifically reliable and applies to the facts in issue. The factors set forth by the Supreme Court are the following:

1. *Testing*. Has the technique or knowledge been tested? The testing would determine accuracy and reliability of the method. If the technique cannot be or has not been tested, it would lack a basic indicia of scientific validity.[62]

2. *Peer review*. Has the technique or knowledge been subjected to peer review and publication? The Court said: "The fact of publication (or lack thereof) in a peer-reviewed journal thus will be a relevant, though not dispositive, consideration in assessing the scientific validity of a particular technique or methodology on which an opinion is premised."[63]

---

60 *See* 509 U.S. 579 (1993).

61 *Id.* at 592–93.

62 *Id.* at 593; for an extensive description of the *Daubert* criteria, *see* MICHAEL R. FONTHAM, TRIAL TECHNIQUE AND EVIDENCE 543–51 (2002).

63 *Id.* at 593–94.

3. *Potential for error*. What is the known or potential rate of error and what standards exist to control the technique's operation?[64] This information permits the court to assess the reliability of the method.

4. *Scientific "acceptance."* As one factor, a court may consider "acceptance" of a technique in a relevant scientific community. "Widespread acceptance can be an i9mportant factor in ruling particular evidence admissible, and 'a known technique that has been able to attract only minimal support within the community' properly may be viewed with scepticism."[65] Thus, the *Frye* test survives as one factor in the new analysis.

Importantly, the U.S. Supreme Court in *Daubert* limited its assessment to the scientific context. Yet, its ruling implies that said factors and observations apply also to other forms of expert testimony.[66] In *Kuhmo Tire Co., Ltd., v. Carmighael*, the U.S. Supreme Court indeed ruled that *Daubert's* requirements that the trial court test reliability and relevance applies to all expert testimony, not just scientific testimony.[67]

In 2000, the U.S. *Federal Rules of Evidence* (FRE) were amended in order to implement the *Daubert* criteria. Rule 702 of these FRE set forth three requirements for the admissibility of expert testimony:

> (a) a fact or data base for the opinion, (b) the use of reliable principles and methods in developing the methods in developing the opinion, and (c) a reliable application of the principles and methods to the facts of the case.[68]

Hence a two-fold reliability requirement forms part of the judicial supervision on (forensic) expert testimony: the court must first determine that an expert has used reliable methods, and, secondly, it must

---

64 *Id.* at 594.

65 *Id.* (citation omitted).

66 *Id.* at 591; *see also* Rehnquist, C.J., concurring and dissenting; *see also* FONTHAM, *supra* note 62, at 545.

67 *See* 526 U.S. 137, 147 (1999); *see* FONTHAM, *supra* note 62 at 545–46.

68 *See* FONTHAM, *supra* note 62 at 549.

determine whether the expert applied the particular method "reliable to the facts of the case."[69]

English courts have also rejected the *Frye* test. However, as will be seen in Chapter 9, the British criminal courts have applied a variation of the *Daubert* doctrine in which certain types of expert evidence are excluded, especially forensic psychiatric and psychology evidence that goes to the reliability of witness statements.[70]

By way of general principle, it could be argued that "where novel scientific evidence is at issue, the additional *Frye* inquiry allows the judiciary to defer to the scientists precisely where to do so recognizes both the need for admissibility of novel scientific evidence where it is sufficiently accepted, and the need to protect against novel scientific evidence which has not even gained general acceptance in the relevant field. The trial court's gatekeeper role under *Frye* involves by design a conservative approach, requiring careful assessment of the general acceptance of the theory and methodology of novel science, thus helping to ensure, among other things, that 'pseudoscience' is kept out of the courtroom."[71]

By way of summary, national and international criminal courts could, when analyzing the evidentiary weight of forensic evidence, apply a two-pronged test, in that they:

(1) identify the field in which the underlying principle falls; and

(2) determine whether that principle has been generally accepted by members of the identified field.

When expert witness opinion presents forensic evidence that is decisive for the particular case, it is important to require corroboration, especially when it concerns a controversial or novel interpretation of scientific data relating either to new techniques (and the general acceptance of such techniques) or even new international crimes.[72] U.S. case law supports this criterion. In rejecting voiceprint evidence, the California supreme court questioned "whether the testimony of a single witness

---

69 *Id.*

70 *See* Spencer, *supra* note 59, at 552–53.

71 *See, inter alia*, State v. Copeland, 922 P.2d 1304, 1314 (Wash. 1996) (*en banc*).

72 For the latter situation, *see* Chapter 9.

alone is ever sufficient to represent, or attest to, the views of an entire scientific community regarding the reliability of a new technique."[73] Similarly, the Pennsylvania supreme court held that the "testimony of one expert . . . cannot satisfy [the *Frye*] standard."[74] As an alternative, one could resort to the approach of the supreme court in the State of New York. Confronted with the complexity of DNA evidence and its powerful impact on a jury or a court, the supreme court set forth a three-pronged test:

(1) Underlying theory must be generally accepted,

(2) Procedures implementing the theory must be generally accepted, and

(3) Testing laboratory must follow these procedures.[75]

In addition to relevance and validity, the reliability of expert opinion is also a crucial issue, the failure of which can lead to a miscarriage of justice. In this regard, it is instructive to consider these factors delineated by the Advisory Committee to the U.S. Federal Rules of Evidence:

(1) whether the underlying research was conducted independently of litigation;

(2) whether the expert unjustifiably extrapolated from an accepted premise to an unfounded conclusion;

(3) whether the expert has adequately accounted for obvious alternative explanations;

(4) whether the expert was as careful as she would be in her professional work outside of paid litigation; and

(5) whether the field of expertise claimed by the expert is known to reach reliable results.

As to criterion (1), it is noteworthy that both the ECHR and the U.S. courts require that expert testimony of general acceptance be given by

73 *See* People v. Kelly, 549 P.2d 1240, 1248 (Cal. 1976).

74 *See* Commonwealth v. Topa, 369 A.2d 1277, 1282 (Pa. 1977).

75 *See* People v. Castro, 545 N.Y.S.2d 985, 987 (Sup. Ct. 1989).

"impartial experts."[76] By way of conclusion, it can be held that "in order to qualify as 'scientific knowledge,' an inference or assertion must be derived by the scientific method. Proposed testimony must be supported by appropriate validation, i.e., 'good grounds,' based what is known. In short, the requirement that an expert's testimony pertain to 'scientific knowledge' establishes a standard of evidentiary reliability."[77]

Yet the reliability and other criteria set out in this section should be established by the parties in criminal proceedings "by a preponderance of proof," which actually implies that the party presenting the expert must show that the expert's findings are based on "sound science."[78] These tests could be applied to retrial proceedings in that new facts, which affect this "sound science," can warrant reopening of a criminal case.

F. THE RIGHT TO HEAR AND CHALLENGE DEFENSE EXPERT WITNESSES UNDER THE ECHR

An assurance that forensic expert evidence is subjected to peer review is instrumental for protection against miscarriages of justice. In this regard, obtaining the attendance and examination of experts on behalf of the defense is crucial, especially in criminal prosecutions, which solely or to a decisive extent are contingent upon forensic evidence. The case law of the European Court of Human Rights (ECHR) lends support to the acceptance of a universal and enforceable right for the defense, independently from the prosecution, to hear its own expert witnesses at trial. Three judgments of the ECHR have shed light on the scope of this right:

In *Bonisch v. Austria*, the European Court held that "literally, sub-paragraph (d) of paragraph 3 [of the European Convention on Human Rights] relates to witnesses and not to experts." Article 6(3)(d) guarantees the right of the accused to examine or have examined the witnesses against him and to obtain the attendance and examinations of witnesses on his behalf under the same conditions as to witnesses against him. The

---

76 *See* ECHR judgments in Bonisch v. Austria, May 6, 1985, ser. A, 92, and Brandtstetter v. Austria, Aug. 28, 1991, ser. A, 211. For these cases *see* Section F; *see* U.S. People v. Kelly, 549 P.2d 1240, 1249 (Cal. 1976).

77 *See* U.S. Supreme Court ruling in the *Daubert* case, *supra* note 60, at 590.

78 *Id.* at 592.

ECHR also contemplates that the principle of arms, inherent in the concept of a fair trial, may require the invocation of a counter-expert, especially when the prosecution's expert plays a dominant role in the criminal proceedings;[79] in this case the Court concluded that this principle was breached.

Brandstetter v. Austria holds that "the mere fact that the expert is employed by the same institute or laboratory as the expert on whose opinion the indictment is based, does not in itself justify fears that he will be unable to act with proper neutrality: to hold otherwise would in many cases place unacceptable limits on the possibility for courts to obtain expert advice." Since the file did not indicate any concrete reason for considering him a witness for the prosecution, the Court held that the principle of equality of arms had not been infringed. Yet no violation of the (overall) right to a fair trial had occurred either, since "the right to a fair trial does not require that a national court should appoint, at the request of the defence, further experts when the opinion of the Court appointed expert supports the prosecution case."[80]

In *Mantovanelli v. France*, the Court interpreted the principle of equality of arms in that it should be effectively endorsed with regard to hearing expert witnesses for the defense. After having stated that one of the elements of a fair hearing, within the meaning of Article 6(1), is the right to adversarial proceedings, the Court first stresses that "compliance with the adversarial principle related to proceedings in a 'tribunal': no general abstract principle may therefore be inferred from this provision that, where an expert has been appointed by a court, the parties must in all instances be able to attend the interviews held by him or to be shown the documents he has taken into account." The crucial observation is that "the parties should be able to participate properly in the proceedings before the 'tribunal'." It is this essential requirement that had not been complied with in the instant case. For, although the Mantovanellis could have made submissions to the Court on the content and findings of the report after having received it, the Court was not convinced that this "afforded them a real opportunity to comment *effectively* on it." The question the expert was instructed to answer was iden-

---

79 *See* Bonisch v. Austria, ECHR, May 6, 1985, ser. A, 92, para. 33.

80 *See* Brandstetter v. Austria, ECHR, Aug. 28, 1991, ser. A, 211, paras. 44–46.

tical to the one the Court had to determine, and pertained to a technical field that was not within the Court's knowledge. Hence, the expert's report "was likely to have a preponderant influence on the assessment of the facts by that court."[81]

The ECHR case law is influential for national jurisdictions even outside Europe. In *United States v. Robinson*[82] it was held that the defense has an independent right to challenge the prosecution evidence whether or not the defense chooses to put forth its own (expert) witness on the issue.

In conclusion, the ECHR pursues the following test as to the position of the defense *vis-à-vis* expert evidence in criminal cases:

(1) Criminal courts must ensure that both prosecution and defense are able to have knowledge of, and (at trial) comment on, the expert evidence of the adversary; and

(2) In the event it is objectively established that the accused has reasons to believe that the particular expert witness is not acting impartially or neutrally in the case at hand, the principle of equality of arms requires that the accused has access to court-appointed counter-experts on his behalf under the same conditions as the prosecution experts.[83]

G. TOWARD A LEGAL STANDARD TO REVIEW FORENSIC OR EXPERT WITNESS EVIDENCE IN CRIMINAL CASES

What criteria should be looked to in adjudicating on potential and asserted errors of forensic sciences or expert witness evidence in criminal cases? I.e., what should be the appropriate legal standard to assess whether or not a miscarriage of justice has been delivered through wrongful expert evidence? In this respect, one could look at the adoption within

---

[81] *See* Mantovanelli v. France, ECHR, Mar. 18, 1997, 1997-II ECHR Rep. 435, paras. 33–36.

[82] 44 F. Supp. 2d 1345 (N.D. Ga. 1997).

[83] For this test, *see also* Petra van Kampen, *Confronting Expert Evidence under the European Conventions*, *in* Harmonisation in Forensic Expertise 201 (J.F. Nijboer & W.J.J.M. Sprangers eds., 2000).

U.S. law of the "abuse of discretion" standard for reviewing a trial court's decision on the admissibility of expert evidence. In *General Electric Corporation v. Joiner*, the U.S. Supreme Court held that the "abuse of discretion" test should be used when appellate courts review decisions with respect to the application of the *Daubert* standard. In the *General Electric* case of 1997, the Supreme Court excluded the plaintiff's expert testimony, saying, "We hold, therefore, that abuse of discretion is the proper standard by which to review a district court's decision to admit or exclude scientific evidence. We further hold that, because it was within the District Court's discretion to conclude that the studies upon which the experts relied were not sufficient, whether individually or in combination, to support their conclusion that Joiner's exposure to PCBs contributed to his cancer, the District Court did not abuse its discretion in excluding their testimony."[84] The abuse of discretion standard may facilitate consistency in that a uniform test can be applied with respect to appellate review of trial court rulings on expert testimony. The "abuse of discretion" doctrine can therefore also serve as a retrial argument in that it could be applied in review cases in the event of new facts that support the invocation of this doctrine in the case at hand. One can say that when the defense is able to establish new facts that the admission of an expert testimony was manifestly unreasonable, a potential retrial argument emerges.

84 *See* 522 U.S. 136, 146–47 (1997).

CHAPTER 9

EXPERT EVIDENCE REQUIREMENTS AND STANDARDS WITHIN INTERNATIONAL CRIMINAL CASES: PROTECTION AGAINST MISCARRIAGES OF JUSTICE

A. INTRODUCTION

With the advent of international and regional criminal courts and the increase of international and non-international armed conflicts, the role of expert witness testimony has gained new attention. In this regard, two salient phenomena emerge: the promulgation of new concepts of international crimes, in anticipation of and in response to such conflicts, and the development by which expert witnesses are more frequently called by prosecution and defense in order to assist the trial chambers of international and internationalized criminal courts in these new areas of international law. Of particular interest in this connection is the Special Court for Sierra Leone (SCSL), which was confronted with two judicially underdeveloped international crimes, one of which is still controversial. These "new" crimes are the conscription of child soldiers and forced marriages. The judges of the Special Court of Sierra Leone specifically accepted forced marriages as an international crime under international customary law.[1]

With this increasing engagement of expert witnesses before international and internationalized criminal courts, fundamental issues arise as to the criteria used to qualify someone as an expert witness and as to the question of when an expert witness is exceeding his or her expertise and entering the province of the judges. This chapter will examine these questions in the light of both common law cases and the case law

[1] *See* Prosecutor v. Brima et al., Case No. SCSL-2004-16-PT, Decision on Prosecution Request for Leave to Amend the Indictment, May 6, 2004.

of the international criminal tribunals, especially several relevant decisions of the SCSL, in order to assess whether and to what extent the expert standards set forth by this jurisprudence is instrumental as to the protection against miscarriages of justice.

B. GENERAL PRINCIPLES PERTAINING TO ADDUCING EXPERT WITNESS EVIDENCE

The purpose of this section is to determine the principles that govern the admissibility of expert witness testimony before international criminal courts, in particular those that have arisen from the law practice of these courts. These principles are frequently invoked by defense counsel acting before international criminal tribunals.

1. Purposes of and Requirements as to Expert Witness Qualifications

a. Common Law Approach

Within common law, the issue of the admissibility of expert evidence, albeit based on a fundamental criterion, is dealt with in a rather undefined way. This approach is aptly contemplated by Lord Justice Lawton in the U.K. case of *R. v. Turner* as follows: "An expert's opinion is admissible to furnish the court with scientific information which is likely to be outside the experience and knowledge of a judge or jury."[2]

In the realm of miscarriages of justice arising from false confessions, the question of whether expert witness testimony is admissible inheres an opinion about the reliability of the particular witness. In 1981, the Court of Appeal in the case of *R. v. Mackinney and Pinfold* came to a negative answer to this question, saying that "whether or not a witness in a criminal trial is capable of giving reliable evidence is a question of fact for the jury."[3] This clearly seems to be an application of the "ultimate issue" rule.[4] This contrasts with the civil law approach, which, in

---

2 *See* 60 Crim. App., R. 80 (1975).

3 *See* 72 Crim. App., R. 78 (1981).

4 *See* Section 3.

the absence of a jury, in principle allows experts to give an opinion about such reliability.[5]

As to adducing evidence on the suggestibility of the accused to intense interrogation methods, common law seems to adopt a more lenient approach. The *Pendleton* case, further discussed in Chapter 7, suggests that the suggestibility in this sense can be subjected to expert opinion.[6]

We will now turn to an inquiry into the boundaries of expert witness testimony before international criminal tribunals, observing that these courts tend to have a more lenient view of the admissibility of expert evidence.

b. The Approach of International Criminal Tribunals

The question and challenge of whether an expert has the requisite qualifications to appear as an expert has received extensive attention before international criminal tribunals. Challenges as to the proper qualifications of a witness who is called as an expert are usually not treated by international criminal tribunals as admissibility issues, but rather as evidentiary issues, i.e., touching upon the evidence.[7] A clear example of this approach may be seen in the decision of the SCSL of August 5, 2005, on the defense motion to the Trial Chamber challenging a prosecution expert witness to testify at trial because of lack of knowledge in the relevant area of expertise.[8]

The defense in that case contested the qualifications of an expert for the prosecution who was called to testify at trial on the novel and highly sensitive topic of "forced marriages." Prior to this testimony, the Trial Chamber of the SCSL had accepted the amendment of the indict-

---

5 *See* the mentioned *Puttense Homicide* case, which led to a reopening in 2001: Dutch Jurisprudence (NJ) 2001, 564.

6 *See* R. v. Criminal Cases Review Commission, *ex* Pendleton [2001] U.K.H.L. 66.

7 *See* RICHARD MAY & MARIEKE WIERDA, INTERNATIONAL CRIMINAL EVIDENCE 199 (2002).

8 *See* Prosecutor v. Brima et al., Case No. SCSL-2004-16-T, Decision on Prosecution Request for Leave to Call an Additional Witness (Zainab Hawa Bangura) Pursuant to Rule 73 *bis*(E), and on Joint Defence Notice to Inform the Trial Chamber of its Position vis-à-vis the Proposed Expert Witness (Mrs. Bangura) Pursuant to Rule 94 *bis*, Aug. 5, 2005.

ment with the additional count of "forced marriages."[9] In particular, the defense held that, according to the resume of the witness in question, her professional background was predominantly that of a "professional insurer." The fact that this witness was also an "internationally renowned activist" in national and international civil society, advocating woman's rights and accountability of governments, would not qualify this witness as an expert in said field.[10] Trial Chamber II of the SCSL rejected this defense argument, holding that: regarding Mrs. Bangura's qualification as "an expert" or lack thereof, we adopt the accepted qualitative definition that "an expert must possess relevant specialised knowledge acquired through education, experience or training in the proposed field of expertise" and the defined role of an expert as being "to assist the Chamber to understand or determine an issue in dispute and the context in which the events took place." We note and accept the Prosecution submissions that despite Mrs. Bangura's educational background being in the field of insurance, her extensive experience is a material factor that qualifies her as an expert with relevant specialised knowledge on the issue of forced marriage during the Sierra Leone conflict.[11]

This rather extensive definition of the term "expert witness" was preceded by a Trial Chamber Decision of the International Criminal Tribunal for Rwanda (ICTR) of May 2, 2005, on the qualification of a prosecution expert. In this oral ruling, the ICTR held that "the role of an expert is to assist the Chamber in understanding the context in which the events took place. The expert must possess a relevant specialised knowledge acquired through education, experience or training in his proposed field of expertise."[12] Thus, the ICTR assessed three sources from

---

9 *See* Prosecutor v. Brima et al., Case No. SCSL-2004-16-PT, Decision on Prosecution Request for Leave to Amend the Indictment, May 6, 2004.

10 *See* Prosecutor v. Brima et al., Joint Defence Notice to Inform the Trial Chamber of its Position vis-à-vis the Proposed Expert Witness Mrs. Banguara Pursuant to Rule 94 *bis*, May 13, 2005, Case No. SCSL-2004-16-T, paras. 6–8.

11 *See* Prosecutor v. Brima et al., Decision of Prosecution Request for Leave to Call an Additional Witness (Zainab Hawa Bangura) Pursuant to Rule 73 *bis*(E) and on Joint Defence Notice to Inform the Trial Chamber of its Position vis-à-vis the Proposed Expert Witness (Mrs. Bangura) Pursuant to Rule 94 *bis*, Aug. 5, 2005, Case No. SCSL-2004-16-T, para. 31.

12 Prosecutor v. Bizimungu et al., Oral Decision on Qualification of Prosecution Expert, May 2, 2005.

which expertise can be derived. The question is whether experience as such, i.e., without education or training as one of the other two sources of expertise, can qualify an individual as an expert. It seems that at the minimum, experience must have a verifiable foundation. Notably, the aforementioned SCSL decision on the issue of expert witnesses clearly shifts the matter of qualification of an expert from an admissibility test to a determination of the weight of the evidence. Paragraph 30 of this ruling says that:

> [i]t is our considered view that all the above concerns are matters that go to the weight and not admissibility of the evidence, and that can adequately be tested during cross-examination. The weight to be attributed to expert evidence will be determined by the Trial Chamber not at this stage but rather at the end of the trial and in light of all the evidence adduced. We also note that in the interests of justice and a fair trial, the Defence are themselves entitled not only to cross-examine Mrs. Bangura but also to submit expert findings to the contrary and to call their own expert witness or witnesses in their defence.

Within international criminal proceedings, there appears to be a tendency to further expand the position of forensic experts in that the qualifications seem to shift to less strict ones. In addition to the case example of the SCSL, one can refer to the ICTR Appeals Chamber judgment in *Prosecutor v. Semanza*, in which case the Appeals Chamber rejected the defense argument to exclude the evidence of an expert witness, holding that the defense misconceived the role of expert witnesses in general. When one reads the reasoning of the Appeals Chamber in this regard, it is clear that it sets forth lenient criteria for expert qualification. The Appeals Chamber holds that:

> the purpose of expert testimony is to supply specialized knowledge that might assist the trier of fact in understanding the evidence before it. Expert witnesses are ordinarily afforded wide latitude to offer opinions within their expertise; their views need not be based upon firsthand knowledge or experience. Indeed, in the ordinary case the expert witness lacks personal familiarity with the particular case, but instead offers a view based on

his or her specialized knowledge regarding a technical, scientific, or otherwise discrete set of ideas or concepts that is expected to lie outside the layperson's ken.[13]

2. Practical Guidelines as to Qualifying and Examining Expert Witnesses

Based on the preceding discussion, it is crucial to develop a checklist that can enable defense counsel to determine an expert's qualification and to conduct a direct examination in order to assess such qualification. This exercise is essential as a safeguard against a potential miscarriage of justice. Improper expert witness testimony may lead to a wrongful conviction, especially if the expert statement plays an important role in the interpretation of the evidence in a criminal case. In this regard, the credibility of the expert is highly relevant and relies on his or her credentials and professional experience.[14] In the context of such a review, two elements should be thoroughly determined:

(1) the expert's general background, including his/her education, degrees, licences and employment history; and

(2) the expert's specific background, including his/her specific knowledge on the situation about which he/she is called upon to testify.

The following general checklist on expert witness qualifications could be used in order to prevent wrongful convictions due to the admission of unqualified expert testimony:

Name

Address

Personal background

Business or occupation: what, how long, description of field, company or organization, capacity, how long at that company or organization, where located, prior positions, description of positions

---

[13] *See* Prosecutor v. Semanza, ICTR Appeals Chamber, judgment, May 20, 2005, ICTR-97-20-A, para. 303.

[14] *See* Thomas A. Mauet, Fundamentals of Trial Techniques 121 (1992).

Education: undergraduate school, degree, when graduated; graduate school. degree, when graduated; area of study

Training: formal courses, what, when, trained under recognized expert?, who, when, how long

Licenses: what, when reviewed, specialty certification, when, requirements

Professional associations: which, positions held

Other background: teaching positions, publications, lectures, consulting work

Expert witness at trials: how many, which side

Experience in specialty: types of examinations commonly done, how many, ever perform a (specify type) test, how many, does that experience include (specify area of expertise relevant to the case at hand)

During these (state number) of years of practice, how many (specify item relevant to the expert's work) have you (bought, sold, dealt with, installed, taken, examined, analyzed, etc.)

During these (state number) of years, what is the total dollar value of all the (specify item relevant to the expert's work) you have (designed, constructed, evaluated, appraised, bought, sold, etc.) (Numbers should show substantial experience, particularly in the specific area involved)[15]

It goes without saying that this list is applicable in both national and international criminal cases.

3. The "Ultimate Issue" Rule Within the Practice of International Criminal Tribunals

The so-called "ultimate issue" rule also serves to protect against miscarriages of justice in the practice of international criminal tribunals. This rule touches upon the question whether an expert may be allowed

---

15 This checklist is derived from MAUET, *supra* note 14, at 121–22.

to give an opinion on the ultimate issue of the case at hand, i.e., to provide an opinion on the very issue that the trial chamber is called upon to adjudicate. The key question here is whether any opinion on the ultimate issue pertaining to an international criminal indictment may assist a trial chamber.[16]

International criminal tribunals have approached the application of this principle, challenged by the defense in cases before the International Criminal Tribunal for the Former Yugoslavia (ICTY) and SCSL, with caution. Two examples will illustrate this.

The ICTY case is that of *Prosecutor v. Kordic and Cerkez*, in which the prosecution sought to tender a report from a military analyst. This report was not founded on the analyst's own observations but rather on secondary sources such as press reports, witness statements, and documents. The defense challenged the tendering of this report as it touched upon the ultimate issue of the case, namely the responsibility of the accused as both civilians and military superiors. The ICTY Trial Chamber upheld the objection of the defense and precluded the report from the evidence because the witness report, without assisting the judges, went into the ultimate issue of the case, the determination of which belonged to the exclusive competence of the Trial Chamber.[17]

Interestingly, the same ICTY Trial Chamber excluded the military expert opinion of a defense witness because it relied only on military evidence; the expert did not visit Bosnia during the conflict but only afterwards, the prosecution was not able to explore the documents and interviews of the defense expert, and this expert made sweeping conclusions without an analysis of all the evidence.[18] The ICTY judges opined that the defense expert's report "purported to deal with the ultimate issue in the case," including questions relating to the responsibility of attacks on various villages and whether these villages were defended.[19] The report, the judges held, did nothing more than simply setting out the defense case rather than being a report of an independent expert.

---

16 *See* MAY & WIERDA, *supra* note 7, at 200.

17 *See* Prosecutor v. Kordic and Cerkez, Transcript, Jan. 28, 2000, 13–89.

18 *Id.*, at 20825–28.

19 *Id.*

In the SCSL case, *Prosecutor v. Brima et al.*,[20] the prosecution introduced a British colonel as a military expert to support its case. This expert wrote a report on the following four issues relating to the Armed Forces Revolutionary Council (AFRC), an organization to which the accuseds allegedly belonged:

(1) the extent to which the organization had a recognizable military hierarchy and structure;

(2) whether the organization had the characteristics of a recognizable military organization;

(3) the level of internal coherence of this organization, more particularly the coherence between strategic, operational, and tactical levels; and

(4) the extent to which the command was effective.[21]

According to the defense, the fourth question directly affected the ultimate issue of the case since the "Further Amended Consolidated Indictment" in *Prosecutor v. Brima et al.* charged the three accused with superior responsibility. In particular the indictment alleged that:

> in addition, or alternatively, pursuant to Article 6(3) of the Statute, [the accuseds], while holding positions of superior responsibility and exercising effective control over their subordinates, are each individually criminally responsible for the crimes referred to in Articles 2, 3 and 4 of the Statute. Each Accused is responsible for the criminal acts of his subordinates in that he knew or had reason to know that the subordinate was about to commit such acts or had done so and each Accused failed to take the necessary and reasonable measures to prevent such acts or to punish the perpetrators thereof.[22]

---

[20] The accuseds, Alex Tamba Brima, Santigie Borbor Kanu, and Brima Bazzy Kamara, were alleged to be members of the AFRC, a body which allegedly overthrew the government in Sierra Leone in May 1997.

[21] Prosecutor v. Brima et al., Transcript, Oct. 12, 2005, at 11 (line 27)–12 (line 8).

[22] *See* Prosecutor v. Brima et al., Further Amended Consolidated Indictment, para. 36.

In view of this, the defense objected to the examination in chief of the military expert on the application of this question and to his characterization of the AFRC as a military organization. It held that, by allowing this, the expert would adduce evidence in chief in regard to the ultimate issue of the case, namely proof of the most prominent of the three requisite elements of command responsibility. The elements required to establish this responsibility include an assessment of whether an accused is in a position of superiority with "effective command and control over subordinates" and knew or had reason to know of their acts, thus establishing the chain of command.[23] The ultimate issue rule prevents an expert witness from testifying on the very matter the judge has to decide and is a fundamental norm of fair justice.

Specifically, defense counsel advanced the following arguments:

> I have several fundamental objections to the line of examination in chief by the Prosecution also regarding the competence of this witness to answer some of these questions. If Your Honours allow me to explain it to you, I think, Your Honours, there are five fundamental points of law which should preclude the Prosecution from examining this witness at least as far as concerns the fourth question of his questionnaire. I will come back to the other three questions.
>
> In my humble submission, Your Honour, the fourth question, which is now put to this witness, goes directly to the ultimate issue of the case. Your Honours are familiar with the decision of the Appeals Chamber in the *Fofana* case of 16 May 2005, paragraph 43 which reads that: "The elements required to establish responsibility under Article 6(3) of the Statute includes an assessment of whether an accused is in a position of superiority with effective command and control over subordinates. That is the first requirement to establish command responsibility."
>
> Your Honours, are also familiar with the fact that the indictment in paragraphs 31 and 36 directly refer to the issue of exer-

---

[23] *See* Prosecutor v. Norman et al., Decision on Appeal Against Decision on Prosecution's Motion for Justice Notice and Admission of Evidence, May 16, 2005, Case No. SCSL-2004-AR73, para. 43.

> cising effective control over their subordinates. That is to be found in paragraph 36 of the indictment. It means that the fourth question which is put to this witness goes directly to the ultimate issue of the case and should, therefore, be excluded from the examination in chief. It also leads to the conclusion that this witness cannot be examined in regard to sections B6 and E5 of the report. . . . There are two precedents from the ICTY which support my submission. The case of the ICTY in *Kordic and Cerkez* resulted in a decision of the Trial Chamber on 28 January 2000. The transcript pages 13289 and 28825 to 20828 [sic] directly relate to the same issue at stake. In that case, Your Honours, the prosecution called a military expert analyst and defence called a military expert. With respect to both experts the Trial Chamber excluded not only the reports of those experts but also their respective testimonies in chief. It is probably illustrative to have a brief look at the ruling of the Trial Chamber with respect to the OTP expert. This expert was drawing conclusions on the very matter upon which the Trial Chamber was required to decide thus invading its province, according to the Trial Chamber.[24]

Counsel continues:

> Here the witness states that judgment will be required and also reference is made to the question of whether effective command was being exercised. Furthermore, the witness has on several occasions in his report given opinion on the issue of military justifications. . . . He clearly and unequivocally says, I quote: "It can be seen that results of the four tests of whether the AFRC [Armed Forces Revolutionary Council] was a military organization in the traditional sense and whether command responsibility exists are . . ." and then he comes up with his conclusions, also referring to commanders. Your Honours, going back now to the rulings of the Trial Chamber of the ICTY, it is interesting to note that in the *Kordic and Cerkez* case, the Chamber excluded the evidence in this regard from a defence expert, reasoning that it totally relied on the defence evidence. Here this witness relied

---

24 Prosecutor v. Brima et al., Transcript, *supra* note 21, at 22 (line 7)–23 (line 18).

> on the evidence of the Prosecution. Second, the witness in that case didn't visit any sites during the conflict himself. Third, in that case the Prosecution was not able to explore the documents and interviews conducted by that expert while writing his report. It is also a similar issue here. Fourth, the Chamber said that this witness merely made sweeping conclusions without an analysis of all the evidence. I think this is also an issue which is under scrutiny here.
>
> Now, the Chamber excluded these expert reports of this military historian saying that it purports to deal with the ultimate issues in the case. That is to be found on page 20825 of the transcript. The Chamber also gave several examples of such issues, and referred to issues relating to the responsibility for attacks on various villages, but also whether these villages were defended; i.e., whether military justifications existed or not. If Your Honours would have a brief look through the report, I think the whole report goes into also the responsibility for crimes. The witness just testified that he was not interested in crime. That was also the ruling by Trial Chamber I in the CDF [Civilian Defense Forces] case, where the same witness was not allowed to testify on any crime matters. Transcript 14807, 14808 and 14765 of the CDF transcript.[25]

Counsel further added:

> And in all regards, the witness is giving opinions on these issues, which can clearly not be seen to be part of his competence. I refer Your Honours also to the rulings of the ICTY, where it said that, "An expert is prohibited to usurp or take over the role of the Trial Chamber, he is not allow to dwell on conclusions or speculate speculations which are clearly outside the scope of his expertise." It is for Your Honours as a Trial Chamber and not for an expert to make factual findings and inferences on the evidence.[26]

25 *Id*. at 26 (line 17)–27 (line 25).

26 *Id*. at 29 (lines 14–23).

Counsel concluded his argument by stating that:

> The Trial Chamber therefore did not accept this report of this military historian as being from an independent source, but a report that simply set out in this instant case a Defence, and that it read like "sustained advocacy and not the independent report of an expert." Finally, Your Honours, there is the decision of the Appeals Chamber in *Delalic et al.* of 20 February 2001, paragraph 594 of the ruling of the Appeals Chamber, where the Chamber said that "an expert opinion is relevant only if the facts upon which it is based are true." "It is for the Trial Chamber and not for the expert to determine whether the factual basis for an expert report is truthful. That determination is made in the light of all the evidence given. Notwithstanding their experience, experts do not have the advantage of that evidence." And if Your Honours take a look at the transcripts of the CDF case where this witness was examined, especially pages 14794 and 14795, the witness clearly accepted that there were inconsistencies, "but I was able to clarify or to form a judgment in my own mind, re-creating the incidents at that time." He used himself the words "re-creating the incidents," and he also accepted that you never get a complete story; you can never have access to everything. That was testified by this witness in the CDF case.
>
> And therefore, Your Honours, based on all these arguments and examples, which are not exhaustive, by the way, I strongly object against the admission of any evidence in chief of this witness which goes to at least the answer to question number 4. . . . In addition, the other sections I just enumerated, all the examples, which go directly to the ultimate issue insofar as it relates to any responsibility for crimes under the current indictment, either AFRC related or to any individual related inclusive of any individual of the RUF [Revolutionary United Front]. Because now, according to this indictment, RUF and AFRC are linked within the concept of a joint criminal enterprise, it is clear that such testimony of this expert will also affect the indictment in this regard.[27]

---

27 *Id.* at 31 (line 21)–33 (line 1).

Trial Chamber II of the SCSL upheld this objection, stating that:

> First of all each of the accused persons in this trial is charged with superior criminal responsibility, as defined under Article 6(3) of the Statute of the Special Court. The elements required to establish this responsibility include an assessment of whether an accused is in a position of superiority with effective command and control over his subordinates and knew or had reasons to know of their acts, *et cetera*, thus establishing the chain of command as an element that is inextricably linked with individual criminal responsibility of each of the accused indictees, which in turn is the ultimate issue, or one of the ultimate issues, in this trial.
>
> We are of the view that the Defence objection raises a fundamental point, which is that what this witness is effectively doing is to provide an opinion or conclusion upon the very matter upon which the Trial Chamber is going to have to rule; namely, whether there was effective command and control appertaining within the AFRC during the period in question when certain acts were allegedly committed, either by the accused persons or their alleged subordinates. We therefore uphold the Defence objection to the question read out at the beginning and rule that the Prosecution cannot ask that question.[28]

Consequently, the prosecutor's expert was exempted from being examined as to the question whether within the AFRC, allegedly a military organization, effective command and control had existed during the period of the indictment.

However, when the prosecution sought to tender the report of this British colonel of August 2005 into the evidence of the AFRC case, the Trial Chamber came to a different conclusion. This decision was preceded by the defense's submissions not to admit this report, on the basis that certain portions thereof were strongly intertwined with the ultimate issue and usurped the role of the Trial Chamber in that the report expressed conclusions on "military justifications" of certain acts. The defense stated that the latter qualifications invaded the Chamber's

---

28 *Id.* at 43 (lines 4–25).

province, as the applicability of certain international criminal law defenses is a matter to be ascertained by the judges. In addition, as advocated by the defense, the military expert's report went into the commission of certain crimes by the AFRC, which clearly fell under the scope of the indictment, such as the allegation of looting and the recruitment of child soldiers. In addition, the issue of diamond mining, as a purported financing source of the AFRC faction, was discussed in the expert report. The defense argued that these references reinforced the violation of the ultimate issue rule. In a second ruling pertaining to this subject, Trial Chamber II of the SCSL admitted the military report into evidence, holding that:

> Rule 89(C) allows the Trial Chamber to admit any relevant evidence. We consider the contents of the report to be relevant and therefore admissible. However, having said that, we shall disregard any material which in our judgment goes to the ultimate issue or provides opinions on matters upon which the Trial Chamber is going to have to rule, or draws any conclusions or inferences which the Trial Chamber will have to draw, or makes any judgments which the Trial Chamber will have to make. With those qualifications, and taking into account that the Defence has had ample opportunity to cross-examine the witness, both on the report and on his sources, we consider that the accused will not be prejudiced by the admission of the report. . . . What weight ought to be attributed to it will be assessed by the Trial Chamber at the end of the trial and in the light of all of evidence adduced.[29]

Thus, the Trial Chamber again qualified this argument as going to the evidentiary weight rather than admissibility.

4. The Applicability Scope of the Ultimate Issue Rule Under International Criminal Law: Individual Criminal Responsibility

Interestingly, the Trial Chamber founded its decision on Rule 89 of the SCSL Rules of Procedure and Evidence (RPE) saying that it may admit any evidence provided it is relevant. The prosecutor had argued

---

[29] *Id.* at 38 (lines 14–29).

that Rule 89 precedes the common-law-based ultimate issue rule when it concerns the "relevance of evidence." This argument raises the question of whether the ultimate issue can be considered as being part of "internationally recognized norms and standards" as enshrined by Rule 72 *bis* (iii) of the SCSL RPE.

In *Prosecutor v. Brima et al.*, the prosecution before the SCSL advanced the argument that a strict application of the ultimate issue rule would not be appropriate before a professional judicial forum, as it was meant to apply to jury trials. It held that forensic experts often testify in domestic trials on ultimate issues, such as the cause of death in a murder case. This overlooks the fact, however, that, even in these domestic examples, the ultimate issue lies with the judiciary or jury. The requisite element for murder is "premeditation," and to this a forensic pathologist cannot and does not testify. In the same vein, a DNA expert can only testify on data detected in a specific case. A DNA expert is not able or allowed to testify whether the DNA donor is also the perpetrator.

As to the jury argument, it is clear that the ICTY Trial Chamber, when it comes to the evaluation of the evidence, does not allow an invasion of its judicial competence to exclusively deal with this, without being assisted by an expert opinion.[30] This may also be deduced from the ICTY Appeal Chamber ruling in *Delalic et al.*, of February 20, 2001, where, faced with the question whether the defense of diminished responsibility applied, it stated that "an expert opinion is relevant only if the facts upon which it is based are true (. . .). It is for the Trial Chamber and not for the (medical) experts to determine whether the factual basis for an expert opinion is truthful (. . .). Notwithstanding their experience, (medical) experts do not have the advantage of that evidence."[31]

It is thus artificial to interpret Rule 98 of the SCSL RPE as an indication that the ultimate issue rule is not part of the criterion of "relevant" evidence. As the ultimate issue rule is intended to protect the independence of the judiciary by making a strict division between assisting a trial chamber on factual matters, which require specific expertise, on the one hand and scrutinizing and weighing the evidence as such, on

---

30 *See Kordic and Cerkez* ruling, *supra* note 17.

31 *See* Prosecutor v. Delalic, Case No. IT-96-21-T, Appeals Chamber judgment, Feb. 20, 2001, para. 594.

the other hand, it should be seen as a peremptory norm of international criminal law, at least insofar as it is meant to prevent an expert from imputing individual criminal responsibility to an accused. Individual criminal responsibility forms the very issue on which the judges of international criminal tribunals have ultimately to decide. It is thus fair to say that it is not the role of any expert to give an opinion on this element.[32]

As a consequence, the calling of expert witnesses to inform the chamber on specific sociological or societal phenomena, which are legally qualified as international "crimes," such as the issues of child soldiers and forced marriages, can probably not be seen as exceeding the competence of the expert or an infringement of the ultimate issue rule. The same is presumably true for a military expert who merely testifies on military structures in general and those within certain organizations specifically. The latter observation can be derived from *Prosecutor v. Brima et al.*, where the SCSL specifically held that "establishing the chain of command is an element that is inextricably linked *with individual criminal responsibility of each of the accused indictees* (emphasis added), which in turn is the ultimate issue, or one of the ultimate issues, in this trial."[33]

C. CONCLUSION: THE ULTIMATE ISSUE AS AN INSTRUMENT IN THE PROTECTION AGAINST MISCARRIAGES OF JUSTICE

Some authors have argued that in international criminal trials, "where there is no need to protect a jury, the question is more often not whether expressions on the ultimate issue should be allowed but whether they assist the court."[34] In this article it was shown that questions, which go into the individual criminal responsibility of individual accuseds, cannot be answered by expert witnesses, as they cannot assist the court in this regard. If experts were permitted to elaborate on this element, it would introduce an artificial and extrajudicial ruling on such responsibilities.

Yet this survey indicates that contemporary international criminal tribunals do allow experts to testify on matters that may affect the evi-

---

32 *See* Prosecutor v. Brima et al., Transcript, *supra* note 21, at 43 (lines 4–25).

33 *Id.* at 43 (lines 12–15).

34 *See* MAY & WIERDA, *supra* note 7, at 200.

dence for proof of the indictment, albeit indirectly, in that experts may give their opinion on particular facts or phenomena based on their professional skills, knowledge, and experience. Examples within international criminal tribunals are the areas of recruitment of child soldiers and forced marriages, insofar as expert opinion does entail informing the court about the content of these areas, rather than the question of individual criminal responsibility.

Overviewing the role of the ultimate issue rule before international and internationalized criminal courts, one may conclude that strict adherence to this rule is instrumental for the protection of the rights of the accused, in that it may prevent improper extrajudicial influence on judicial independence.

To maintain the judiciary's impartiality, the institution must have a variety of internal mechanisms to prevent any undue influence by external sources. When one allows expert witnesses to invade the judicial province, the independent mind of the court is endangered. Even though international and internationalized criminal tribunals are comprised of professional panels, the exclusion of expert evidence on this issue remains essential in order to ensure public respect for the courts and the maintenance of the transparency of the judicial process. Of course, the key question is: what is the ultimate issue? This will inevitably call for a case-by-case approach based on an analysis of the indictment in each case. Sometimes a grey area may be entered. For instance, is it possible for a military expert to testify about command responsibility within a military organization to which the accused allegedly belonged without testifying specifically about the accused person him or herself? Can the ultimate issue rule be infringed in the event the expert indirectly adduces evidence on the issue of command responsibility while this issue forms one of the liability modes of the indictment? It is clear that the boundaries of the ultimate issue rule within international or internationalized criminal trials are far from established.

CHAPTER 10

NEW AND CHANGING EXPERT EVIDENCE: BASIS FOR RETRIALS IN INTERNATIONAL CRIMINAL CASES?

The complex and ambiguous position of forensic experts within international and domestic criminal trials, as elaborated in the preceding chapter, has a reverse side. In principle, for a retrial application to be successful, new, fresh evidence should be produced, in that new facts or new evidence of a factual nature should be adduced. It remains to ask whether a changing opinion of forensic evidence or a new expert witness report, based on the same facts as presented at trial, may be advanced as a successful retrial argument in criminal cases. In this regard, the case law of the British Criminal Cases Review Commission (CCRC) is illustrative, and may serve to inform other criminal law systems and even international criminal proceedings. Two decisions illuminate how this subject may be approached.

The first of these is the *Gilfoyle* decision of December 20, 2000, in which Gilfoyle was convicted for the murder of his wife. The defense argued that Gilfoyle's wife committed suicide by hanging herself. The jury did not accept the probability of suicide, based upon the testimony of a forensic expert that it was unlikely that the wife, who was pregnant, hanged herself. After the conviction, another forensic expert challenged the testimony of his colleague, saying that it was unclear whether this case involved suicide or murder.

The CCRC referred the case to the Court of Appeal, which held that the initial conviction was not unsafe on the basis of the following reasoning: "Granting that the new pathological evidence is neutral, in that it indicates that suicide is as equally likely as homicide, the decision as to which was the cause of death, now as at trial, depends on the non-pathological evidence. If that evidence proves, as in our judgment it plainly does, because that is the inevitable inference, that the appellant killed the deceased, it is immaterial precisely how he killed her."[1] Importantly, the Court of Appeal leaves open the possibility that the changing or new opinion of a forensic expert, based on the very same facts as adduced at trial, can constitute a retrial argument and render the initial conviction unsafe.[2]

Another example is the British *Brown* case, which was reopened in 2001. In 1996, Brown was sentenced to seven years imprisonment for sexual abuse of the five-year-old son of his girlfriend. Two medical experts examined the boy and concluded that there was inconclusive evidence of sexual anal penetration. Yet a third and well-renowned medical expert came to an opposite finding. The jury in its conviction was led by this third expert conclusion. In 1997, Brown applied to the CCRC, which engaged three new experts to look into the medical evidence. The experts concluded that indications to contradict anal penetration were neglected, such as the absence of blood or bruises (as well as emotional problems), whereas the boy's suffering from diarrhea could explain his anal wounds. Based on these new medical findings, the CCRC referred the case to the Court of Appeal, which overturned Brown's conviction, holding that "it now has to be recognized that what was found is capable of a number of explanations. The medical evidence raises questions which may be difficult to answer, but that very fact undermines one of the main pillars of the prosecution case."[3]

In conclusion, it may be said that a changing or new forensic expert opinion as such, even when it is not accompanied by new factual (medical) evidence, may, under certain circumstances, facilitate a retrial in criminal cases. Especially when the evidence relies mainly, or to a decisive extent, on forensic expertise or interpretation by expert witnesses, it is more likely and justifiable to reconsider a conviction. Hence, depending on the pillars of the prosecution case, this retrial avenue should be scrutinized.[4]

---

1 R. Criminal Cases Review Commission, *ex* Gilfoyle, Dec. 20, 2000, Case No. 990180053, para. 38, *available at* www.ccrc.gov.uk.

2 In some civil law systems, such as in the Netherlands, such a situation does not in principle lead to a retrial, although, under stringent conditions, an exception is allowed by the Dutch Supreme Court; *see* Judgment of this Court of 26 June 2001, NJ 2001, 564.

3 R. v. Criminal Cases Review Commission *ex* Brown, Jan. 22, 2001, Case No. 2001/4928/C4, para. 27.

4 This is also the approach of the Dutch Supreme Court; see its Judgment of June 26, 2001, NJ 2001, 564 in the landmark case, known as the *Puttense Homicide* case; *see further* Chapter 12.

CHAPTER 11

PROCEDURAL MECHANISMS *SUI GENERIS* AGAINST MISCARRIAGES OF JUSTICE

A. BALANCING THE PREVENTION OF WRONGFUL CONVICTION: JUDICIAL ECONOMY AND EQUALITY OF ARMS WITHIN INTERNATIONAL AND INTERNATIONALIZED CRIMINAL TRIALS[1]

This chapter will examine several procedural mechanisms *sui generic*, which may be instrumental in both the prevention and redressing of miscarriages of justice. The first mechanism discussed in this section focuses on two procedural principles that may lie at the basis of miscarriages of justice.

1. Introduction: Converging Objectives Before International Criminal Tribunals

The preservation of the principle of equality of arms is critical for the rule of law and indispensable to a law-based society. Nowadays, this principle, as derivative of the overarching right to a fair trial, has attained the status of a fundamental human right. On the international plane, the legal-political environment, in which international and internationalized criminal courts function, brings greater attention to the credibility of these institutions. To maintain this credibility and integrity, these institutions must endorse several procedural mechanisms to ensure that trials are conducted in accordance with the principle of equality of arms. Because the prevalence of the principle of equality of arms is instrumental in the protection of the individual rights of accused persons, it is an indispensable safeguard against abuse of powers, as well as a guarantee that separation of powers will be maintained.

---

1 This section by the author was published in 29 FORDHAM INT'L L.J. (2006) 201-29.

International and internationalized criminal courts are comprised of organs and parties with competing interests. Several principles applicable before these institutions can result in antagonistic positions and situations from the perspective of the defense acting before these fora. Moreover, the question merits thought as to whether such antagonistic processes may fuel wrongful convictions.

Recent practice before the ICTY reveals a tension between the principle of equality of arms and that of judicial economy. Although the latter does not have the same human rights standing as that of equality of arms, it is rooted in the Rules of Procedure and Evidence (RPE) of international and internationalized criminal courts. For instance, Rule 73 *ter* of the ICTY RPE endows the Trial Chambers of this *ad hoc* international criminal tribunal with the authority to limit the length of time and number of witnesses allocated to the defense case.[2]

This chapter considers the trend to effectuate judicial economy within international criminal trials as it relates to the principle of equality of arms from the standpoint of the defense. It focuses on this juxtaposition as exemplified in the contemporary case law of the ICTY. In addressing this position, the analysis in this article will build on the assumption that the inter-relationship between these two notions must be interpreted in the light of two cardinal parameters: the protection of the interests of the defense, and the principle of independence and non-political use of the notion of judicial economy.

2. Ensuring Equality of Arms on the International Plane: Defense Scope and Limitations

On the international plane, the synergy between judicial economy and equality of arms is of perennial importance to ensure a fair trial. Central to the principle of equality of arms is that the defense in criminal cases is not unjustly put at a disadvantage compared to the position of the prosecution in terms of time and facilities to prepare its defense. The defense must also have access to information that is material to the

---

[2] *See also* Rule 73 *ter* (C) and (D) of the RPE of the ICTR, and Rule 73 *ter* (C) and (D) of the RPE of the SCSL; *see*, in general, for judicial economy, Daryl A. Mundis, *From Common Law Towards Civil Law: The Evolution of the ICTY Rules of Procedure and Evidence*, *in* 2 LEIDEN J. INT'L L. 367–82 (2001).

case. The European Court on Human Rights (ECHR) has repeatedly stressed that the basis of a fair trial, as enshrined by Article 6(1) of the European Convention, is that criminal proceedings should be adversarial and that there should be equality of arms between the defense and the prosecution.[3] The ECHR has interpreted the latter element as encompassing the requirement that both parties must be given the opportunity to have knowledge of, and to comment on, the observations filed and the evidence adduced by the other opponent.[4]

In the context of the ICTY, on the issue of equality of arms, the Appeals Chamber has accepted that "the principle of equality of arms between the prosecutor and the accused in a criminal trial goes to the heart of the fair trial guarantee."[5] The ICTY Appeals Chamber judges have held that, at a minimum, "equality of arms obligates a judicial body to ensure that neither party is put at a disadvantage when presenting its case," particularly when it concerns procedural equity.[6] So far, however, international criminal tribunals have not accepted the thesis that equality of arms should also extend to financial resources. This principle has therefore not been interpreted as encompassing the approach that prosecution and defense should have equal access to financial means to prepare and present their case.[7] The question is whether the neglect of such an approach complies fully with human rights norms. In the case of *Steel and Morris v. U.K.*, the ECHR was confronted with a denial by the British authorities of free legal assistance to two London Greenpeace associates who accused the McDonald's restaurant chain of "economic imperialism," i.e., destruction of rainforests and exploitation of children. Charged in the United Kingdom with a libel suit (instigated by McDonald's), Steel and Morris petitioned for free legal assistance. This request was rejected, since, at that time, such assistance was not provided for in libel cases within the U.K. system. As a consequence, the two defendants were compelled to represent themselves in a procedure that took 313 daily court sessions during which 130 witnesses were heard

---

3 *See* Judgment of the ECHR, June 24, 2003, Dowsett v. United Kingdom; Edwards and Lewis v. United Kingdom, Judgment, July 22, 2003.

4 *See* ECHR in Brandstetter v. Austria, Judgment, Aug. 28, 2001.

5 *See* Prosecutor v. Tadic, Case No. IT-94-1-A, Judgment, July 15, 1999, para. 44.

6 *Id.*, paras. 48, 50; *see also* ICTY Appeal Chamber, Prosecutor v. Oric, Interlocutory Decision on Length of Defence Case, Case No. IT-03-68-AR73.2, para. 7.

7 *See* Prosecutor v. Ojdanic, Final Assessment of the Accused Ability to Remunerate Counsel, Case No. IT-99-37-PT, June 23, 2004.

and 40,000 pages of evidence were adduced. Following their conviction by U.K. judges, Steel and Morris appealed to the ECHR, saying that the U.K. proceedings were conducted in contravention of the principle of equality of arms relative to the absence of free legal assistance. In its judgment of February 15, 2005, the ECHR upheld this complaint, saying that there was an unacceptable "inequality of arms" in that the underlying procedure was complex and a considerable imbalance existed between the defense resources of Steel and Morris, on the one hand, and McDonald's, on the other.[8] Accordingly, the ECHR held that Article 6 of the European Convention on Human Rights had been violated.

Thus, the above considerations are relevant not only to equality of arms on the procedural level, but also with respect to equality in financial terms. An application for free legal assistance implies the absence of financial resources to pay one's defense. Such absence should be incompatible with the fair trial requirement of international criminal trials, particularly the rationale of the principle of equality of arms, insofar as it would undermine the effectiveness of the defense.[9]

These developments make it both important and timely to take a closer look at the impact of the notion of judicial economy on the fair trial rights of accuseds within international and internationalized criminal proceedings.

3. Concurrence of Equality of Arms and Judicial Economy in the Law Practice of the International Criminal Tribunals

a. The Practice of the International Criminal Tribunals: A Shift to Controlling the Effectiveness of the Proceedings

Before looking into the emerging concurrence between the notion of judicial economy and that of equality of arms, it is important to examine the contents of the former principle. Both before international and internationalized criminal tribunals, particularly before the ICTY, the

---

8 ECHR, Steel and Morris v. U.K., Judgment, Feb. 15, 2005, Application No. 68416/01. *See*, for this judgment and implications in further detail, GEERT-JAN ALEXANDER KNOOPS, THEORY AND PRACTICE OF INTERNATIONAL AND INTERNATIONALIZED CRIMINAL PROCEEDINGS 42–49 (2005).

9 *See* further Section A.4.

ICTR, and the SCSL, a shift in the trial practice is discernible, resulting in a greater emphasis on the supervisory role that the trial judges may play in controlling the proceedings.[10] It may be observed that, while the first trials before the ICTY were mainly dominated by common law principles, more recent practice reveals a more intense level of control of the proceedings by the Trial Chambers comparable to the level of judicial control during the criminal proceedings in the civil law traditions.[11] It is clear that this shift and process result from the perception of the international community that trials at the ICTY and ICTR have become too lengthy. Consequently, it is felt that this situation may be addressed by attributing to the Trial Chambers more authority to control the proceedings.[12] As observed by Daryl Mundis, this development has been ongoing, under the rubric of improving case management, at least since the 18th plenary of the ICTY judges in July 1998.[13] As a result, both the amendments of the Rules of Procedures and Evidence (RPE) and trial practice before the ICTY and ICTR no longer endorse a system primarily driven by the parties, typical for common law jurisdictions, but rather one in which the (pre-)trial judges feature in a more dominant and active role, comparable to the *juge d'instruction* in civil law jurisdictions.[14] Two examples will suffice.

Two amendments were made to Rule 90 of the ICTY RPE, which governs witness testimony, in order to enable the Trial Chamber to exercise more control over the mode and order of examining witnesses and presenting evidence. In particular, Rule 90(G) was added, empowering the Trial Chamber to ascertain the truth and "avoid needless consumption of time." Rule 90(H)(i) was added in order to enable the judges to restrict cross-examination to subjects covered in the opposing party's direct examination, unless the Trial Chamber extends the scope of the cross-examination. Rule 90(H)(ii) was enacted in order to avoid the necessity of recalling witnesses who can provide evidence relevant to the case for the cross-examining party.[15]

---

10 *See also* Mundis, *supra* note 2, at 367.

11 *Id.* at 368.

12 *Id.*

13 *Id.*

14 *Id.* at 368–69.

15 Rule 90(H)(ii) reads: "(ii) In the cross-examination of a witness who is able to give evidence relevant to the case for the cross-examining party, counsel shall put to

A second example of this tendency towards a civil law oriented form of judicial control and economy may be seen in the promulgation of Rules 73 *bis* and 73 *ter*, which rules clearly envision pre-trial case management.[16] Sub-paragraph (C) of these Rules enables the Trial Chamber to reduce the number of witnesses if the Trial Chamber considers the expected testimony to be cumulative. In effect, these sub-rules attribute to the Trial Chambers wide powers as to how the parties decide to present and prove their cases. These mechanisms clearly represent a form of judicial control designed to "economize" the trials in a way similar to civil law traditions.[17]

In this context, it is worth noting that similar considerations on effective case management and judicial economy have been promulgated by the judges of the International Criminal Court (ICC). Pursuant to Article 52 of the ICC Statute, the 18 ICC judges have drawn up regulations in order to implement the ICC Statute and the RPE of the ICC. These regulations will be crucial to the "routine functioning" of the ICC and the conduct of trials.[18] Even more than the judges of the ICTY and ICTR, the ICC judges are endowed with considerable (investigative) autonomy and power to control the proceedings.[19] In line with the notion that the ICC judges will play an active role in running the trials is their incentive to also intensively manage the cases that are before the Court. An example of this judicial role as to the case management of ICC trials can be found in Regulation No. 54 of the ICC regulations. This regulation entails a list of orders the ICC Trial Chamber may issue while organizing the trials. Such orders, which clearly include an endorsement of judicial economy, can extend to:

(1) the length and content of legal arguments and the opening and closing statements;

---

that witness the nature of the case of the party for whom that counsel appears which is in contradiction of the evidence given by the witness." *See* Mundis, *supra* note 2, at 372.

16 *See* Mundis, *supra* note 2, at 372.

17 *Id.*

18 *See* Regulations of the Court, Doc. ICC-BD/01-01-04 (May 26, 2004); *see*, for these regulations, Hans-Peter Kaul, *Construction Site for More Justice: The International Criminal Court after Two Years*, 2 AJIL 375–79 (2005).

19 *See* Kaul, *supra* note 18, at 376.

(2) a summary of the evidence the participants intend to rely on;

(3) the length of the evidence to be relied on;

(4) the length of questioning of the witnesses;

(5) the number and identity (including any pseudonym) of the witnesses to be called;

(6) the production and disclosure of the statements of the witnesses on which the participants propose to rely;

(7) the number of documents as referred to in Article 69, paragraph 2, or exhibits to be introduced together with their length and size;

(8) the issues the participants propose to raise during the trial;

(9) the extent to which a participant can rely on recorded evidence, including the transcripts and the audio-record of evidence previously given;

(10) the presentation of evidence in summary form;

(11) the extent to which evidence is to be given by an audio or video link;

(12) the disclosure of evidence;

(13) the joint or separate instruction by the participants of expert witnesses;

(14) evidence to be introduced under Rule 69 as regards agreed facts;

(15) the conditions under which victims shall participate in the proceedings; and

(16) the defenses, if any, to be advanced by the accused.

The items under (1), (3), (4), and (7) directly relate to "economizing" the trials. Judicial economy was clearly one of the parameters in the drafting process of the ICC regulations. In doing so, the ICC judges, while implementing the practical experiences of the ICTY and ICTR, pursued the following objectives:

(1) to streamline trials as far as possible;

(2) to avoid, as much as possible, long and detailed, and possibly insufficiently substantiated, indictments with a multitude of alternative or cumulative charges that would have to be decided separately in the course of the trial;

(3) to limit the average length of trials as far as possible;

(4) to avoid crafting judgments extending to hundreds of papers;

(5) to prevent, where possible, trials from being hijacked by the defendant, for example through the option of judicial appointment of defense counsel; and

(6) to protect, above all, the rights of the accused and the defense, including the accused's right to trial without undue delay in accordance with Article 67, paragraph 1(c).[20]

These developments make it clear that judicial case management of international and internationalized criminal trials, fueled by judicial economy motives, is becoming an ever more important objective of the judges of these courts. A difficulty that may arise, however, concerns the way in which this development restricts fair trial rights, particularly constraining the principle of equality of arms.

b. Challenging Judicial Economy and Prioritizing Equality of Arms: The *Oric* Case

In the law practice of international and internationalized criminal courts, several situations come to mind in which competing interests emerge between equality of arms and the notion of judicial economy. In *Prosecutor v. Oric*, the Appeals Chamber of the ICTY, confronted with such a situation, gave priority to the principle of equality of arms. In the *Oric* case, after the prosecution closed its case, the defense served notice of its intention to call 73 witnesses, estimating that the defense exami-

20 *See*, for these objectives, *id*. at 376–77.

nation in chief would take 249 hours. The prosecution in the *Oric* case had called 50 witnesses and had taken roughly 260 hours of court time. The Trial Chamber rejected the proposed framework of the defense case. It held that a number of areas of evidence had been "sufficiently addressed during the prosecution case in a manner and to an extent which in the Trial Chamber's opinion does not require any further evidence on the part of the defense." Specifically, it held that the following areas were sufficiently addressed:

> The historical and political background which led to the armed conflict in Bosnia-Herzegovina in April 1992;
>
> The large number of attacks by Bosnian Serb forces on Bosnian Muslim villages within the geographical scope of the indictment, including the wanton destruction and plunder of Bosnian Muslim villages and hamlets and the laying of mines by Bosnian Serb forces in and around destroyed Bosnian Muslim villages and hamlets;
>
> The killing and inhumane treatment of Bosnian Muslims, whether civilians or non-civilians, by Bosnian Serbs or Bosnian Serb forces;
>
> The policy of 'ethnic cleansing' by Bosnian Serb political or military authorities before, during and after the crimes charged in the indictment, in and around Srebrenica;
>
> The positive treatment of Serbs—whether civilians or non-civilians, hostages or wounded, in Bosnian Muslim hospitals—by Bosnian Muslims, unless relating to persons identified in Counts 1 and 2 of the Indictment;
>
> The situation of Srebrenica during the period relevant to the Indictment, namely the positioning of Bosnian Serb forces in and around Srebrenica, and the isolation of Srebrenica from the rest of Bosnia and Herzegovina while being under constant siege and suffering from air and artillery bombardment;
>
> The influx of refugees in Srebrenica and the critical condition under which the population of Srebrenica had to live during the period relevant to the indictment, to include food and medical

shortages, hygiene issues, security concerns, sporadic electricity and telecommunications shortages;

The genocide committed against Bosnian Muslims in Srebrenica in 1995;

The military superiority of the Bosnian Serbs at the time relevant to the Indictment, namely that the Bosnian Serbs were better equipped militarily than the Bosnian Muslims and that, in addition, the Bosnian Serbs benefited from the support of the former JNA and from Serbia;

The extent of the dependence of Bosnian Muslim Military capacity in Srebrenica on weapons that could be captured from the Bosnian Serb forces; and

The urgent necessity for Bosnian Muslims to attack villages and hamlets named in the Indictment in order to try and secure food, medicine and weapons, for the purpose of the survival of the Muslim population in Srebrenica. (This limitation does not in any way mean that the Trial Chamber does not require any further evidence that the Defence may wish to adduce in relation to the aspect of military necessity to engage in wanton destruction as alleged in Counts 3 and 5 of the Indictment).[21]

In addition, the Trial Chamber rejected the defense proposal on grounds that the defense case could be concluded with a much shorter presentation of evidence than the schedule proposed by Oric. As a result, the Trial Chamber ordered Oric to file a new witness list with no more than 30 witnesses and ordered that the defense case had to be finished within two months. Accordingly, the prosecution heard 50 witnesses in chief over 100 days, while the defense was only allotted 30 witnesses over 27 days. Thus, the defense in the *Oric* case was faced with two forms of restrictions fueled by judicial economy views: restriction of the subject matter of the scope of the defense case, and restriction of the number of defense witnesses and duration of the defense case. Both restrictions

---

21 *See* Prosecutor v. Oric, Trial Chamber Decision on First and Second Defence Filings Pursuant to Scheduling order, July 4, 2005, Case No. IT-03-68-T, para. 4.

were set aside by the ICTY Appeals Chamber upon an appeal by the defense against these limitations.[22]

The next sections will address the reasoning of the Appeals Chamber in light of the overall consequences of its decision for the applicability of the principle of equality of arms within international criminal proceedings.

c. Equality of Arms as a Human Rights Protection Against Judicial Economy Before International Criminal Tribunals

Article 6(1) of the ECHR and Article 14(1) of the ICCPR both delineate the right to a fair trial without explicitly mentioning the principle of equality of arms. Yet, according to the case law of the ECHR, this principle forms part and parcel of the overarching notion of a fair trial.[23] As previously noted, the ICTY Appeals Chamber in *Prosecution v. Tadic* adopted this view, holding that "the principle of equality of arms between the prosecutor and accused in a criminal trial goes to the heart of the fair trial guarantee."[24] Although no overall definition is to be found on any of the human rights instruments, it is accepted that, at a minimum, "equality of arms obligates a judicial body to ensure that neither party is put at a disadvantage when presenting its case."[25] Within the case law of the international criminal tribunals, it seems also accepted that the principle of equality of arms only encompasses procedural equity, rather than equity in financial resources between prosecution and defense.[26] Yet, the seriousness of the charges and complexity of the criminal case are of great importance in determining the extent to which the principle of equality of arms may apply in a certain case.[27] Because proceed-

---

22 *See* Prosecutor v. Oric, Interlocutory Decision on Length of Defense Case, July 20, 2005, Case No. IT-03-68-AR73.2.

23 *See* Prosecutor v. Tadic, Appeals Chamber Judgment, July 15, 1999, Case No. IT-94-I-A, mentioned in paras. 48–50.

24 *See id.*, para. 44; *see also Prosecutor v. Oric, supra* note 21, para. 7.

25 *See Prosecutor v. Tadic, supra* note 23, paras. 48, 50.

26 *See generally* about this interpretation, KNOOPS, *supra* note 8, at 42–49.

27 *See* Decision of Human Rights Committee in *Phillip v. Trinidad and Tobago*, Communication No 594/1992, Views of the UNHRC, Oct. 20, 1998 [1998] IIHRL 123 (Oct. 20, 1998), in which it was held that the ability for the defense to prepare a mur-

ings before international criminal tribunals involve the most serious crimes, as well as extremely complex criminal cases when compared to domestic criminal cases, equality of arms is of perennial importance to ensure the fairness of international proceedings. The ICTY Appeals Chamber in the *Tadic* case acknowledged this, holding that "under the Statute of the International Tribunal, the principle of equality of arms must be given a more liberal interpretation than that normally upheld with regard to proceedings before domestic courts."[28]

This implies that the principle of equality of arms should be subjected to teleological interpretation depending on the nature of the criminal proceedings at hand, rather than construed on a rigid and pre-fabricated notion, such as a presumption that *ab initio* it would extend to equity in financial resources. Accordingly, its human rights protection underlies a flexible and nuanced approach, balancing the accused's position against the prosecution interests and those of judicial economy on a case-by-case basis.

d. Equality of Arms: Practical Consequences for the Position of Defense Before International and Internationalized Criminal Tribunals

As to the practical implications of the human rights dimension of the principle of equality of arms, the ICTY Appeals Chamber has set forth some guidelines, which are also of importance for future cases before international and internationalized criminal tribunals.

Equality of arms, in terms of time and witness allocation to the defense, according to the interpretation of the ICTY Appeals Chamber judges, does not imply that an accused "is necessarily entitled to precisely the same amount of time or the same number of witnesses as the Prosecution."[29] The principle of equality of arms is functionally interpreted by the ICTY Appeals Chamber in view of the specific tasks and functions of the parties within an international criminal trial. This is

---

der case during one weekend prior to the commencement of the trial amounted to a violation of the principle of equality of arms.

28 *See Prosecutor v. Tadic, supra* note 23, para. 52.

29 *Id.*, para. 7.

expressed in the following way: "The Prosecution has the burden of telling an entire story, of putting together a coherent narrative and proving every necessary element of the crimes charged beyond a reasonable doubt."[30] The defense position and defense strategy concentrate "on poking specifically targeted holes in the Prosecution's case, an endeavor which may require less time and fewer witnesses."[31]

Hence a guideline emerges, namely that of the principle of proportionality, which governs the interpretative scope of the principle of equality of arms as to both the defense and prosecution position. In paragraph 7 of the *Oric* case, it is said that "a principle of basic proportionality, rather than a strict principle of mathematical equality, generally governs the relationship between the time and witnesses allocated to the two sides." The criterion here is that of "reasonable proportionality."[32]

The Appeals Chamber promulgates a teleological interpretation of those procedural rules, which are meant to endorse judicial economy within international criminal trials. Particularly, in the context of Rule 73 *ter* of the ICTY RPE, which gives the Trial Chamber the authority to limit the length of time and number of witnesses allocated to the defense,[33] the Appeals Chamber held that "such restrictions are always subject to the general requirement that the rights of the accused pur-

---

30 *Id.*

31 *Id.*

32 *Id.*

33 Rule 73 *ter* reads:

(A) Prior to the commencement by the defence of its case the Trial Chamber may hold a Conference.

(B) In the light of the file submitted to the Trial Chamber by the pre-trial Judge pursuant to Rule 65 *ter* (L)(ii), the Trial Chamber may call upon the defence to shorten the estimated length of the examination-in-chief for some witnesses. (Amended 17 Nov 1999, amended 12 Apr 2001)

(C) In the light of the file submitted to the Trial Chamber by the pre-trial Judge pursuant to Rule 65 *ter* (L)(ii), the Trial Chamber, after having heard the defence, shall set the number of witnesses the defence may call. (Amended 17 Nov 1999, amended 12 Apr 2001)

(D) After commencement of the defence case, the defence may, if it considers it to be in the interests of justice, file a motion to reinstate the list of witnesses or to vary the decision as to which witnesses are to be called. (Amended 12 Apr 2001)

(E) After having heard the defence, the Trial Chamber shall determine the time available to the defence for presenting evidence. (Amended 12 Apr 2001)

suant to Article 21 of the Statute of the International Tribunal[34] be respected."[35] To establish the teleological element in this interpretation—that of assessing the reasonableness of the time and facilities allocated to the defense in preparing its case in terms of "reasonable proportionality"—an objective standard or test has to be applied by the Trial Chambers. In this connection, paragraph 8 of the *Oric* decision says that, in determining this reasonableness, "a Trial Chamber must also consider whether the amount of time is *objectively* adequate [emphasis added] to permit the accused to set forth his case in a manner consistent with his rights."

As to the question of what "reasonably proportional" implies, the Appeals Chamber interprets this criterion on the basis of the content of the particular case and thus seems to combine the restrictions of subject matter and the number of witnesses and the duration of the case. In paragraph 9 of the *Oric* decision, the Appeals Chamber judges require that, in this regard, the trial judges take into account the complexity of the remaining issues as to the subject matter of the (defense) case in order to permit the defense "a fair opportunity to present [its] case."

The element of the complexity of the subject matter of the case, as an argument that triggers equality of arms more predominantly, seems especially to arise when specific defenses are at stake. In the *Oric* case, the defense intended to hear witnesses pertaining to the defense of military necessity. This implies that an inherent disproportion between the prosecution and defense, in terms of allocation of time and witnesses, can become unreasonable when a rather complex defense is to be raised by the accused. In the *Oric* case, the Trial Chamber allotted the accused only 30 witnesses and 27 days of testimony, whereas the prosecution was allocated time to hear 50 witnesses over 100 days of testimony. The Appeals Chamber concluded that this allotment to the defense was "not remotely proportional to the time that was allotted to the prosecution." This disparity is especially flagrant "given the complexity of the issues

(F) During a trial, the Trial Chamber may grant a defence request for additional time to present evidence if this is in the interests of justice. (Amended 12 Apr 2001)

34 Which article virtually sets forth the fair trial guarantees of Article 14 of the International Covenant on Civil and Political Rights (ICCPR).

35 *See Prosecutor v. Oric, supra* note 21, para. 8.

at stake, particularly regarding military necessity" so that "such disproportion cannot be justified."[36]

Consequently, restrictions imposed by the Trial Chamber, as to the subject matter the defense wishes to address in its case, should be extensively interpreted and assessed in light of the "reasonableness" of the defense case. Although the trial judges, under Rule 73 *ter*, have discretionary power to restrict the subject matter scope of the defense case, such restrictions should be limited in the event the defense has unsuccessfully applied for an acquittal under Rule 98 *bis* of the ICTY RPE[37] based on a certain substantive argument or defense. In paragraph 6 of the *Oric* decision, the Appeals Chamber held that (judicial economy) limitations of the subject matter of the defense case, imposed by the Trial Chamber in the *Oric* case were "unreasonable in light of the fact that the defense of military necessity may play a central role in Oric's defense on counts 3 and 5 of the indictment." As to the relevance of Rule 98 *bis* in this context, the Appeals judges opined that:

> unless the Trial Chamber decides in his favor on those counts and issues a formal acquittal under Rule 98 *bis*, there is simply no way to justify restricting Oric from presenting information regarding, at a minimum:
>
> — the military situation, broadly construed, throughout the Srebrenica region, including the placement of Bosnian Serb forces, equipment, and artillery; the isolation of Bosnian Muslim forces; and the alleged military superiority of Bosnian Serbs at the time relevant to the indictment
>
> — The allegedly desperate situation of the region's Bosnian Muslim population
>
> — The alleged reliance of Bosnian Muslims on weapons that could be captured from Bosnian Serb forces

---

36 *Id.*, para. 9.

37 Rule 98 *bis* reads: "At the close of the Prosecutor's case, the Trial Chamber shall, by oral decision and after hearing the oral submissions of the parties, enter a judgement of acquittal on any count if there is no evidence capable of supporting a conviction."

— Any facts that could cast non-trivial doubt on the credibility of prosecution witnesses

In overviewing the *Oric* decision, one can say that, in this way, Rule 98 *bis* may provide the defense an important procedural mechanism to limit the exercise and applicability of judicial economy pursuant to Rule 73 *ter*.

4. Equality of Arms *Vis-à-Vis* Investigation and Documentary Evidence

a. Equality in Resources, Logistics, and Investigations: Practical Consequences for Defense Before International Criminal Tribunals

Equality of arms in financial terms, i.e., the ability for defense lawyers to have access to sufficient funds, was addressed in the ICTY case *Prosecutor v. Milutinovic et al.* In that case, the defense was seized of a confidential "motion for additional funds" filed by the defense of Dragoljub Ojdanic seeking an order directing the registrar to allocate additional funds for pre-trial preparation. The defense held that several particularities justified such additional funding: the scope of the case, the nature of the accused's defense, and the extended and complex legal issues involved. The Trial Chamber of the ICTY, in its "Decision on Motion for Additional Funds" of July 8, 2003, denied this motion, saying that, while accepting the Registrar's position that it is open to a certain flexibility in considering requests for additional resources, the defense "should demonstrate exceptional circumstances or circumstances beyond its control if such requests are to be granted." The judges held that no such circumstances were ascertained. In particular, two arguments were advanced by the Trial Chamber for this ruling:

(1) First, it reasoned that the current legal aid system of the ICTY, which provides for a flat fee (lump sum) for the pre-trial stage for all indigents accused before the ICTY, taking into account the complexity of the cases, should be interpreted in light of both the need to ensure full respect for the rights of all indigents accused and the efficient use of the limited resources of the ICTY's legal aid system.

(2) Second, the Tribunal held that counsel who have agreed to represent indigents accused before the ICTY "are fully aware of the system of remuneration for assigned counsel, including the basis for calculating the costs of legal representation . . . and the maximum allotment for the pre-trial stage according to the particular circumstances of the case"

Therefore, within the systems of the ICTY and ICTR, the principle of equality of arms apparently has a different connotation and meaning when it comes to equality of means and resources. The ICTR is quite explicit on this matter, saying that equality between the parties as a fundamental right "shall in no way be interpreted to mean that the Defence is entitled to the same means and resources as available to the Prosecution."[38]

The practical consequences of this approach were envisioned by the "Interim Report on the SCSL" of April 2005 issued by the War Crimes Studies Center of the University of California at Berkeley. On page 14 the following paragraphs (subheaded "Defence, Equality of Arms") draw the attention:

> The court's own website defines equality of arms as a "reasonable equivalence in ability and resources of Prosecution and Defence." In practice, these two branches of the court are quite different in terms of their administrative structures and available resources: unlike the independent OTP [Office of the Prosecution], the Defence Office falls under the umbrella of the Court Registry. Employees of the OTP are salaried employees of the Court, whereas defence teams are independent contractors who bill hourly, subject to the oversight of the Principal Defender. Although the Prosecutor stated that he does not believe the resource allocation between the prosecution and the defence is unfair, some members of the defence have questioned whether the principle of "equality of arms" is being meaningfully upheld at the Special Court.

---

[38] *See* Prosecutor v. Kayishema and Ruzindana, ICTR Judgment May 21, 1999, para. 60.

> In light of the prosecution's burden of proof, it would be inappropriate to make direct comparisons in all instances to determine the adequacy of funds afforded the Defence Office and the individual defence teams. While the Special Court is not strictly bound by the precedents of the *ad hoc* tribunals, it frequently takes guidance from judgments and rulings from the ICTY and ICTR, and the ICTR has established that "equality of arms . . . does not necessarily amount to the material equality of possessing the same financial and/or personal resources." Even when applying the standard of "reasonable equivalence" adopted by the court, however, the Principal Defender and members of some defence teams were able to give examples of where they felt the defence was clearly prejudiced: areas of particular concern included disparities in logistical support, such as transport and office resources, as well as discrepancies in investigation and expert witness budgets.

As to the question whether equality is ensured with respect to logistical support and investigations, the Berkeley report contains the following clarifications:

> (i) Logistical Support.
>
> While the Principle Defender noted that some conditions for defence counsels had improved fairly consistently during her time in office, the current conditions under which the Defence Office and the defence teams operated were still thought to be less than adequate. Some defence teams alleged that the office resources afforded to the defence were minimal when compared with the OTP; which in some cases hampered the ability of teams to effectively prepare for trial. The Registrar has noted that the defence teams at the Special Court were perceived to be comparatively as well equipped or more equipped than their counterparts at the *ad hoc* tribunals. However, the court's own benchmark of "reasonable equivalence" is not based on an inter-tribunal comparison, but on how resources are shared within the institution of the court itself. Although many of the specific needs of the defence have been and are continuing to be addressed, there is a broader perception within the defence that the prosecution has access to substantially greater material advantages.

(ii) Investigators.

The use of investigators in international tribunals forms a pivotal part of both the prosecution and the defence cases. Investigators from the OTP's investigations section have worked closely with the OTP's legal team to refine target lists, establish leads and uncover the background to crimes committed during the Sierra Leonean conflict to provide the OTP with the information it needed to draft the first indictments and through the prosecutions phase. Some of them will continue to assist the prosecution during the defence's case and the rebuttal case at the trial stage. Investigators from the defence teams are charged with following up on the veracity of the statements and testimony of OTP witnesses, establishing leads for potential defence witnesses, and recovering any evidence that may further support the relevant defence team's case. While it is fair to expect that the investigation resources allocated to the prosecution would exceed that of the defence, the discrepancies between the two budgets have been raised as an "equality of arms" concern by some members of the defence. The Defence Office has advocated for the addition of international investigators and lengthier contracts for national investigators.

According to information received from the Principal Defender, the Defence Office budget for investigations for fiscal year 2004/05 was less than half the amount allotted to the OTP for investigation-related travel alone. However, the Registrar has commented that as prosecution cases draw to a close, more emphasis will be placed on the defence budget. The recently released budget for fiscal year 2005/6 reflects this shift: defence travel for investigations is approaching its equivalent in the OTP budget, and the investigations budget is more than double that of the previous year. The Registrar seems to have adopted a pragmatic and malleable approach to defence budgeting given the constraints within which he is working, and in some instances the Principal Defender has been provided with the flexibility to shift funds from one area of the budget to another.

Although some members of the defence continue to express dissatisfaction with the way in which resources are allocated

> within the court, the Registry has attempted to remain in an ongoing responsive relationship to the needs of the defence. The existence of the Defence Office itself is a novel development, which, if managed effectively, could amount to a significant gain for the recognition of the rights of the accused in international criminal tribunals.[39]

These comments are reinforced by the Human Rights Watch report titled *Justice in Motion: The Trial Phase of the Special Court for Sierra Leone*, published in November 2005.[40] The conclusions of this report as to the issue of having access to resources reveal several areas of concern from the perspective of equality of arms for defense:

> Despite these advances, funding of two areas essential to the preparation and presentation of defense cases—expert witnesses and international investigators—may prove insufficient. Defense counsel and court staff told Human Rights Watch that they believe that currently allotted amounts for the defense expert witness budget for 2005–2006 are inadequate. The Defence Office requested approximately three times what was ultimately allotted in the 2005–2006 budget for defense consultants and experts. While the notion of equality of arms between the prosecution and defense does not mean precise equality of resources, it is notable that substantial disparities exist between financial allotments for the defense and prosecution in this area.[41]

Similar concerns can be derived from this report as to the ability for defense teams to have access to defense investigators:

> Defence Office staff and defense counsel have expressed similar concern about lack of funding for investigators. Prior to its April 2005 mission, Human Rights Watch was told that access to investigators by defense teams has improved over time, with defense teams having access to the full-time assistance of national investigators plus limited access to the assistance of an interna-

39 *See Interim Report on the Special Court for Sierra Leone*, Apr. 2005, U.C. Berkeley War Crimes Studies Center, at 14–15.

40 *Available at* http://www.hrw.org/reports/2005/sierraleone1105/.

41 *Id.*, at ch. IV.A.

tional investigator. Given the importance of investigation to preparation of the defense, and ongoing demands for investigation as additional information is disclosed throughout trial, the opportunity to secure some assistance of international investigators is significant. Consistent with these developments, the Defence Office requested funds for 2005–2006 to cover the services of an international investigator for up to two months for each defense team, in addition to the full-time services of national investigators. However, the 2005–2006 budget allots less than half the amount the Defense Office requested for investigators.

When Human Rights Watch researchers raised concerns over the limited allocations for defense expert witnesses and investigators in April 2005 in Freetown, we were told that the budget does not necessarily reflect the total amount that may be made available for all areas; some areas may extend into the next budget cycle and there may also be funds remaining from the previous budget cycle, which ended on June 30, 2005. In follow-up discussions, Human Rights Watch was also told that the budget is constructed based on anticipated amounts, but that there is flexibility; funds can be found to address needed areas and there is a commitment by the court to ensuring reasonable needs by the defense. Human Rights Watch was also told that the principal defender has been invited recently to meet with Registry staff to discuss needs in these two areas so that any appropriate redeployments can be considered.

Detailed budgeting for all potential operational needs throughout the court is a difficult task, especially when resources are scarce. However, particularly with the departure of the court's first registrar, Robin Vincent, relying on the flexibility of the Registry to ensure adequate funding for key areas for the defense poses some concern.[42]

Therefore, this Human Rights Watch report recommends that adequate funding on the areas of both defense investigators and expert witnesses should be endorsed.

---

42 *Id.*

Although it is clear that the prosecutorial burden of proof before international criminal tribunals may, to some extent, justify a higher budget as opposed to that of the defense, the fundamental nature of equality of arms as a human rights principle must at least be interpreted as ensuring an approximate equality in financial terms.[43] The inference from the fact that the prosecution is required to meet the requisite burden of proof may not amount to a substantial imbalance in financial, logistical, and investigative resources between the parties.[44] After all, putting a defense case before an international criminal tribunal requires that the defense is able to invoke its arguments and establish criminal law defenses by a "preponderance of evidence."[45]

b. Equality of Arms and Access to Documents of Governmental or International Organizations

Can the principle of equality of arms be affected by the accessibility of the defense to potentially exculpatory materials in possession of governments and international organizations? Quite often, the prosecution is given access to such materials, while the defense lacks the same powers.[46] Such a situation arose before the SCSL with respect to detention and military records of one of the accused in possession of the governmental authorities of Sierra Leone. Disclosure thereof could have been decisive in establishing an alibi defense of the accused. The Trial Chamber of the SCSL, confronted with absence of cooperation on the part of the military authorities of the government of Sierra Leone, issued an order that the government provide the defense with these documents. The defense, in its underlying motion, relied heavily on the principle of equality of arms.[47] Ultimately, access to these materials was given on the basis of Rule 54 of the RPE.[48]

---

43 *See* Richard May & Marieke Wierda, International Criminal Evidence 271 (2002).

44 *Id.*

45 For this burden, *see* Geert-Jan Knoops, Defenses in Contemporary International Criminal Law 225–28 (2001).

46 *See* May & Wierda, *supra* note 43, at 271.

47 *See* SCSL-2004-16-PT, Kanu—Decision on Defence Motion in Respect of Santigie Borbor Kanu for an Order under Rule 54 with Respect to Release of Exculpatory Evidence, June 1, 2004.

48 Rule 54 reads: "At the request of either party or of its own motion, a Judge or

In *Prosecutor v. Simic*, the ICTY proceeded on this issue by granting the defense access to ICRC materials that had been disclosed only to the tribunal and prosecution. The ICTY relied upon Article 21(1) of its Statute, which states that all persons shall be equal before the Tribunal.[49]

Yet, an imbalance between the parties before international criminal tribunals seems to persist. For instance, the agreement between the United Nations and the government of Sierra Leone[50] provides in Article 17(1) that "The Government shall cooperate with all organs of the Special Court at all stages of the proceedings. It shall, in particular, facilitate access to the Prosecutor to sites, persons and relevant documents required for the investigation." Yet, the fact that this agreement only provides that the government of Sierra Leone is obliged to "facilitate access to the Prosecution to sites, persons and relevant documents required for the investigation," without including the position of the defense, implies that the defense has no independent position comparable to the prosecution when it concerns having access to sites, persons, and relevant documents required for the defense case. Therefore, the defense before the SCSL is not entitled to have direct access to witnesses on the same footing as the prosecution. In order to ensure equality of evidentiary sources and cooperation, it is crucial that international criminal tribunals assume an active role in redressing this inherent imbalance.[51]

5. Pitfalls and Dangers of Judicial Economy Within International Trials

Human rights courts and committees have developed a rather sophisticated view on the scope of the principle of equality of arms from the defense perspective. For international and especially internationalized

---

a Trial Chamber may issue such orders, summonses, subpoenas, warrants and transfer orders as may be necessary for the purposes of an investigation or for the preparation or conduct of the trial."

49 *See* Prosecutor v. Simic, Decision on Application by Stevan Todorovic to Re-Open The Decision of July 27, 1999, Feb. 28, 2000, para. 29; *see also* Prosecutor v. Kordic and Cerkez, Order for the Production of Documents by the European Community Monitoring Mission and its Member States, applying the principle of equality of arms.

50 Agreement between the United Nations and the Government of Sierra Leone on the Establishment of a Special Court for Sierra Leone, Jan. 16, 2002.

51 *See* MAY & WIERDA, *supra* note 43, at 272.

or mixed criminal tribunals, the assessment of the boundaries of this principle is relatively new. In particular before the latter tribunals that have a restricted life span, such as the SCSL and Khmer Rouge Tribunal (KRT), the notion of judicial economy, pressured by these time-limited mandates, and that of the principle of equality of arms for the defense will present a conflict.

Internationalized criminal tribunals operate with limited budgets and low levels of external commitment. Thus, their effectiveness can be questioned.[52] This implies that considerable pressure will be exerted on these tribunals to complete their tasks within the prescribed time limits imposed by the international community. It is observed that these tribunals require substantial commitments of funds, voluntarily donated by states, as well as qualified personnel and political will, to contribute to international criminal justice.[53] Hence, the principles of judicial economy and that of equality of arms are sure to collide within proceedings before internationalized courts. The essential question is whether the former notion should necessarily prevail over the latter due to the time limits in the life span of these courts. Judicial economy is sometimes motivated by the argument that international trials should be conducted without undue delay. This argument is, however, a moot one.

First of all, the legal status of the notion of judicial economy cannot be equated with that of equality of arms, the latter being qualified as a fundamental human rights notion enshrined by Articles 6(1) of the ECHR and 14(1) of the ICCPR. Second, the pursuit of judicial economy, in that defense rights are restricted as in the *Oric* case, can ultimately affect the legitimacy of international and internationalized criminal trials.[54] As noted by Daryl Mundis, "Efforts to further limit the choices of the defense, as a means of improving effective case management, should be pursued only with great caution, since they have a potential to seriously hinder the right of the accused to a fair trial pursuant to Articles 20 and 21 of the (ICTY) Statute."[55]

---

52 *See* Sylvia de Bertodano, *Current Developments in Internationalized Courts*, 1 JICJ 244 (2003).

53 *Id.*

54 *See* Mundis, *supra* note 2, at 370.

55 *Id.*

6. Equality of Arms Before International and Internationalized Courts: A Structural Inequality?

It may be said that equality of arms in its full scope will probably never be achieved, as the financial procedural and investigative facilities allocated to prosecution and defense are structurally and inherently unequal when it concerns trials before international and internationalized tribunals. This is apparent in at least three ways.

First, in most cases the prosecution is enabled to start its investigation and take witness statements one to two years prior to the issuance of an indictment. The defense comes into play only after a considerable amount of evidence and material has already been assembled. Mindful of the different responsibilities and tasks of prosecution and defense in an international criminal trial, it cannot be denied that this situation amounts to a disadvantage for the defense, especially when the defense faces an accused who pleads not guilty.

Second, in particular with respect to trials before internationalized courts meant to adjudicate on regional conflicts such as in Sierra Leone and East Timor, one of the fundamental problems the defense faces lies in the structural disadvantage in gaining effective access to witnesses dispersed over the provinces. Most often, in this type of conflict, the prosecution has the power and resources to initiate outreach programs much earlier than the defense. Outreach programs focus on dissemination to the wider public, especially those civilians living in the provinces of a region or country affected by a conflict, of the purposes and function of a specific international or mixed tribunal established to try international crimes related to that conflict. In this way, prosecution and defense may obtain cooperation of witnesses to build their cases. For instance, before the SCSL, specific budgets are allocated to the prosecution and defense to conduct outreach programs throughout the whole territory of Sierra Leone. However, the prosecution was enabled to effectuate these outreach programs as of 2002, while the defense teams, which were appointed in mid-2003, were first able to set up programs more than a year later. Thus, the defense teams of the nine detainees before the SCSL were *de facto* put in a disadvantageous position as to the effectiveness of outreach programs. Since the prosecution had a considerable time advantage—more than a year—considerable numbers of witnesses had already been approached and enlisted for the prosecution's case.

Third, in terms of staffing and financing international and internationalized criminal courts, a structural inequality can be clearly seen. For instance, the budget report on the Registrar of the SCSL 2005–2006 comprises a staffing table for each organ of the SCSL.[56] The total number of prosecution members is 45, including 18 investigators, whereas the Defense Office is staffed with 11 individuals, excluding the defense lawyers who are contracted to represent the nine detainees. Every defense team, in principle, has the right to contract one investigator, as opposed to the 18 investigators on which the OTP may rely. Of course, it can be argued that the OTP has to deal with the investigation in nine cases, which are currently pending before the SCSL. However, this does not take away the imbalance with respect to the position of the defense, especially when (as is the case) prosecution investigators may share the information from the various cases, and prosecution trial attorneys before the SCSL repeatedly use the same witnesses in different trials.

The responsibilities of international criminal tribunals may impose conflicting pressures on both the offices and the judges. This pressure may produce a stalemate. To establish such tribunals for the sake of justice on a pre-determined budget risks having, in the end, no justice delivered in terms of endorsing fair trial rights. Yet, the alternative of not vesting such tribunals bears the risk of having no justice delivered at all. Thus, a formidable challenge rests on the international community responsible for the establishment of these tribunals, to contemplate the consequences of these conflicting pressures in order to achieve a fair application of the principle of equality of arms.

7. Conclusions: Safeguard Against Politically Motivated Application of Judicial Economy and Wrongful Convictions

Both the notions of judicial economy and that of equality of arms are indispensable to the proper conduct of international and internationalized criminal trials. Yet, unlike the former notion, the principle of equality of arms represents a more structural and fundamental safeguard

---

56 *See* SCSL Budget 2005–2006, version 05/06, at 7.

to facilitate a fair trial at this level. Preservation of and respect for equality of arms, at the minimum in procedural sense, does not depend on endorsement of judicial economy, at least from the perspective of defense fair trial rights. The dichotomy between the principle of equality of arms and the notion of judicial economy remains largely undetermined by the case law of the international and internationalized criminal courts, notwithstanding the Appeals Chamber ruling in the *Oric* case. This ruling brought some clarification as to the fair trial limitations of the "asymmetric" effect of "judicial economy" for the defense, particularly in terms of equality of arms. This clarification provides important guidance regarding the interpretation of the Rules of Procedure and Evidence that are promulgated to ensure judicial economy policy.

Yet, current practice before international and internationalized criminal courts cannot take away the fear about a politicized and non-independent application of such rules, seen from the perspective of the defense. The best way to resolve this fear is, on a case-by-case basis, to review these particular rules and interpret them not in a literal manner but rather from the perspective of the protection of human (defense) rights. A broad interpretation of Rules of Procedure and Evidence pertaining to the concept of judicial economy, such as Rule 73 *ter* of the ICTY RPE, carries the risk that such norms may potentially be used as a tool to prioritize the political agendas of member states or the United Nations as to the budgetary restraints and mandates pertaining to international and internationalized criminal tribunals. Accordingly, such an approach increases the risk for miscarriages of justice. The preliminary purpose of the principle of equality of arms is therefore to reduce the risk of politically motivated applications of the concept of judicial economy and may, in this way, attribute to the prevention of wrongful convictions.

B. THE ABUSE OF PROCESS DOCTRINE IN INTERNATIONAL LAW: A PROSPECTIVE REMEDY TO PROTECT AGAINST MISCARRIAGES OF JUSTICE

1. Introduction

A second procedural mechanism *sui generis* in this area is rather underdeveloped but at the same time relevant for law practice. Miscarriages of justice can occur in the event prosecutorial behavior seriously circumvents basic defense rights of the accused, for instance by withholding exculpatory evidence, or by prosecuting solely, or to a decisive extent, on political or discriminatory grounds. A combination of such proceedings may heavily prejudice the accused and may diffuse the truth-finding process before national and international courts. As a result, these abuses of the judicial process and errors of fact may provoke a wrongful conviction. In this section, a specific doctrine, i.e., that of abuse of process, will be assessed as a prospective remedy developed within international law, under which criminal courts are empowered to stay criminal proceedings. It will be observed that this doctrine can be instrumental in preventing miscarriages of justice when abuses contaminate the criminal proceedings while prejudicing the defense rights of the accused.[57]

2. The Abuse of Process in the Practice of International Criminal Courts

The abuse of process doctrine as a means to redress potential wrongful convictions was initially enunciated by common law judges in a variety of situations. Basically, exclusion of evidence and even a stay of proceedings is imposed in the event:

(1) admission of evidence would have an adverse effect on the fairness of the proceedings;[58] or

(2) law enforcement authorities are (in)directly implicated in serious misconduct, in which case a stay of criminal proceedings can be ordered.

In common law, this remedy has been applied when an accused was kidnapped abroad, in order to circumvent existing extradition obligations

---

[57] *See* for this doctrine, in general, G.J. ALEXANDER KNOOPS, SURRENDERING TO INTERNATIONAL CRIMINAL TRIBUNALS: CONTEMPORARY PRACTICE AND PROCEDURES 235–43 (2002); Antonio Cassese, *Effective Remedies for Abuse of Process in General International Law, Treaty Law and the Russian Legal System*, unpublished paper (2004).

[58] *See* Lord Hofman, in House of Lords, R. v. Loosely, *available at* http://www.parliament.the=stationery-office.co.uk/pa/ld200102/ldjudgmt/jd011025/loose=2.htm, para. 36; R. v. Shannon [2001] W.L.R. 51, 68.

toward the foreign officials who acted jointly with U.K. officials.[59] Although the rationale of staying proceedings is that a continuation of prosecution would shock the public conscience,[60] it is fair to say that this remedy contributes to the prevention of wrongful convictions in that it helps avoid errors of fact. An example is the case that led to the ECHR judgment in *Teixeira de Castro v. Portugal*, in which situation law enforcement agencies provoked an individual to commit a crime he otherwise would never have committed. The ECHR concluded that no fair trial could have been held in the instant case and held that Portugal, in pursuing criminal proceedings, irremediably violated Article 6(1) of the European Convention on Human Rights.[61]

At the international level, the doctrine of abuse of process has also been adopted as a remedy to sanction serious misbehavior on the part of prosecutorial or investigative authorities that prejudice fundamental defense rights. In particular, two decisions delivered by international criminal tribunals have promulgated this doctrine within international criminal trials.

The first example is the ICTR Appeals Chamber decision in *Prosecutor v. Barayagwiza* of November 3, 1999, in which accumulation of infringements of procedural rights occurred, among them a failure to hear a writ of *habeas corpus*, challenging the legality of the continued detention of the accused. The Appeals Chamber held that a stay of proceedings based on the doctrine of abuse of process was justified.[62] The judges of the ICTR Appeals Chamber opined that the rationale of this doctrine is to ensure the public interest in the integrity of criminal proceedings, especially as a safeguard for the fundamental rights of an accused.[63] The Court stressed that the application of this doctrine should be determined on a case-by-case basis, leaving a Trial Chamber with considerable discretionary power as to the legal consequences thereof.

---

59 *See* House of Lords, R. v. Horseferry Road Magistrates' Court, *Ex Parte* Bennett, 1 A.C. 42 (1994); *see also* State v. Ebrahim, Judgment South Africa SC (Appellate Division) Feb. 11, 1991, *reprinted in* 31 I.L.M. 896 (1992).

60 *See* Cassese, *supra* note 57, at 26.

61 *See* Judgment June 9, 1998, Application No. 25829/94.

62 *See* Prosecutor v. Bagarayagwiza, Case No. ICTR-97-19-AR72, Judgment, Nov. 3, 1999.

63 *Id.*, paras. 74–77.

In the case at hand, the ICTR Appeals Chamber ordered the release of the accused and dismissal of the indictment with prejudice.[64]

A second example of the application of the abuse of process doctrine before an international criminal tribunal was established by both the Trial Chamber and Appeals Chamber of the ICTY in *Prosecutor v. Nikolic*.[65] In that case the accused was forcibly taken by unknown persons and removed from Serbia to Bosnia, where he was handed over to NATO forces (SFOR) and subsequently transferred to the ICTY. The accused challenged the jurisdiction of the ICTY and sought to dismiss the indictment based upon the abuse of process doctrine. Both the Trial Chamber and the Appeals Chamber upheld this doctrine, although it was rejected in the case at hand. Both decisions are instructive in that they set forth a rather high threshold.

In its Decision on Defense Motion Challenging the Exercise of the Tribunal of October 2, 2002, the ICTY Trial Chamber rejected the defense argument that proceedings with the trial would undermine the integrity of the judicial process.[66] Yet, the judges added that in order to apply this doctrine, "it needs to be clear that the rights of the accused have been *egregiously* violated [emphasis added],"[67] which standard was not met by the accused, especially when considered in proportion to the serious war crimes charges.

Although it supported the Trial Chamber's rejection of the defense argument, the ICTY Appeals Chamber adopted the abuse of process doctrine in this case, formulating the basis as follows:

> Although the assessment of the seriousness of the human rights violations depends on the circumstances of each case and cannot be made *in abstracto*, certain human rights violations are of such a serious nature that they require that the exercise of jurisdiction be declined. It would be inappropriate for a court of law to try the victims of these abuses. Apart from such exceptional

---

64 In its decision of March 31, 2000, the ICTR Appeals Chamber, based on a review request of the Prosecution relating to new facts as to the role of it in the procedural failures, reversed its earlier judgment in that it no longer dismissed the charges.

65 *See* Case No. IT-94-2-T.

66 *Id.*, para. 111.

67 *Id.*

> cases, however, the remedy of setting aside jurisdiction will, in the Appeals Chamber's view, usually be disproportionate. The correct balance must therefore be maintained between the fundamental rights of the accused and the essential interests of the international community in the prosecution of persons charged with serious violations of international humanitarian law.[68]

Although in the above-mentioned cases the doctrine of abuse of process is not explicitly framed as a mechanism to prevent miscarriages of justices in terms of errors of fact, it seems tenable that, ultimately, this doctrine is beneficial in protecting against potential miscarriages of justice. After all, egregious violation of fundamental defense rights may taint the credibility of the evidence and ultimately the truth-finding process.

3. The Abuse of Process Doctrine in Relation to Miscarriages of Justice in International Criminal Law Practice

Exclusion of evidence or a stay of proceedings as remedies for abuse of process, as current case law within international criminal law indicates, may apply whenever abuses or malpractice on the part of the investigating or prosecutorial authorities are so serious and so detrimental to the rights of an accused that a subsequent trial would be severely tainted and, in fact, result in a miscarriage of justice.[69] In these instances the likelihood of a serious contamination of the criminal proceedings should be excluded by a prospective remedy to anticipate a wrongful conviction. This may happen when the court finds, for instance, that the investigating or prosecuting authorities have deliberately or negligently withheld exculpatory evidence to the detriment of the accused, a situation which occurred in *R. v. Kamara*.[70]

Within common law, another example of the application of this doctrine emerged in the *Twitchell* case. Twitchell was initially convicted of manslaughter and armed robbery, mainly on the basis of his own con-

---

[68] *See* Prosecutor v. Nikolic, Appeals Chamber Decision, June 5, 2003, Case No. IT-94-L-S, para. 30.

[69] *See* Cassese, *supra* note 57, at 20.

[70] For this case, *see* Chapter 6.

fessions. Prior to his trial, he withdrew his confessions claiming that these were obtained through torture by police officers. An inquiry did not support his allegations. A few years after his conviction, another accused, Treadaway, was able to prove, in a civil suit against the U.K. government, that he had suffered harm from torture practices conducted during an interview with the West Midlands Serious Crime Squad, the same police squad that had undertaken the investigations against Twitchell. In addition, the alleged torture method, i.e., putting the head of the accused in a plastic bag to prevent him from breathing, matched that of the purported method Twitchell spoke about. The CCRC referred the *Twitchell* case to the Court of Appeal for a new trial on the basis of its finding that "subsequent findings against police officers involved in the appellant's case, coupled with the similarity of misconduct, demonstrates a system of corrupt and dishonest conduct by officers of the West Midlands Crime Squad such as to render the convictions unsafe."[71] Accordingly, the Court of Appeal quashed Twitchell's conviction on the basis of the conclusion that "we make no findings in this appeal about individual officers. We rely on findings made by Mackinnon J in relation to the *Treadaway* case, and the other material, which (. . .) gave rise to findings or admissions on which reliance can properly be place for the purposes of this appeal. On this basis, highly significant and potentially devastating cross-examination could plainly have been directed to Brown, Taylor, Perkins and Quin, in the light of what is now known about those officers."[72] Importantly, Twitchell's conviction was considered "unsafe" on evidence obtained in another case, which approach amounts to a rather extensive view of the criterion "new evidence."

At the international level, such a situation arose in *Prosecutor v. Blaskic*, in which case the ICTY Appeals Chamber, confronted with failure to disclose exculpatory evidence to the defense, i.e., three exhibits, did not allow for a stay of proceedings.[73] Rather, the ICTY judges found that the defense had not suffered any material prejudice as a result and declined to sanction the prosecution.[74] Yet, the Appeals Chamber stressed

---

71 R. v. Criminal Cases Review Commission, *ex* Twitchell, Oct. 26, 1999, Case No. 9800326/S2.

72 *Id.*, para. 48.

73 *See* Prosecutor v. Blaskic, Case. No. IT-95-14-T-A, Appeals Chamber Judgment, July 29, 2004.

74 *Id.*, para. 299.

that the prosecution bears an obligation to establish procedures designed to ensure that, particularly in instances when the same witnesses testify in different cases, the evidence provided by such witnesses is re-examined in light of Rule 68 to assess whether any material must be disclosed.[75] Yet the basic notion set out in this paragraph is that, although the abuse of process doctrine is not expressly aimed at prevention of errors of fact within criminal proceedings, it is tenable that it may have this effect. Accordingly, this doctrine should be accorded weight as a remedy to prevent or redress miscarriages of justice, i.e., wrongful convictions in a factual sense.

4. Conclusions

This section has shown that international law has developed a general principle to remedy serious violations of the right to a fair trial or the right to due process. The abuse of process doctrine is a derivative of this general principle. It serves to invalidate acts resulting from grave malpractice by law enforcement officials, admonish those officials, or impose a relatively light sentence on the defendant. In more serious cases, courts may go so far as to dismiss the indictment. Generally speaking, courts enjoy judicial discretion in this matter. It is for them to decide the specific remedy, based on the individual circumstances of each case and the severity of the authorities' misconduct. However, international law provides general parameters guiding the use of that discretionary power:

(1) the seriousness of human rights violations by law enforcement agencies;

(2) the extent to which these violations undermine the integrity of process by restricting or jeopardizing the right of the individual concerned to a fair administration of justice; and

(3) the need for the remedy to be proportional to the seriousness of misconduct.

The more serious the human rights violation and the greater its negative impact on the integrity of the process, the more radical the remedial action that may be taken by a court. It follows that in the most serious

75 *Id.*, para. 302.

instances of prosecutorial misconduct, courts are legally bound to resort to the most drastic remedy, that is, dismissal of the indictment.[76]

As a consequence of this doctrine, criminal trials may be reviewed and reopened on the basis of this doctrine, presupposing that such investigative or prosecutorial misconduct was only revealed after the criminal trial came to an end. Thus, the abuse of process doctrine constitutes an important procedural mechanism for defense counsel in the realm of redressing miscarriages of justice, not only at the level of international criminal cases but also within domestic criminal proceedings.

C. CROSS-EXAMINATION INSTEAD OF WRITTEN EVIDENCE IN INTERNATIONAL CRIMINAL CASES AS PROTECTION AGAINST MISCARRIAGES OF JUSTICE: THE ICTY EXAMPLE

Another procedural mechanism *sui generis* relates to the extent to which cross-examination in criminal case will be allowed and the relation between this technique and written evidence. In most civil law jurisdictions, a judge may enter convictions in criminal cases on the basis of "dossiers," i.e., on the basis of written evidence or testimony.[77] The question is whether such an approach makes a criminal law system vulnerable to miscarriages of justice, given that witnesses may not appear in court, and the evidence can be admitted on the basis of their written statements taken down by police officers. Balancing the interest to expedite criminal trial proceedings against the rights of the accused, as well as the prevention of miscarriages of justice within domestic criminal cases, recourse may be had to the approach promulgated by Rule 92 *bis* of the ICTY/ICTR RPE.[78] This rule endorses procedures for proof of facts other than by oral evidence, both by the prosecution and defense. Confronted with the dilemma of when to admit written instead of oral evidence for reasons of judicial economy, paragraph (a) of this rule allows a trial chamber to admit written evidence of a witness in lieu of oral testimony only when it goes to the proof of a matter other than the acts and conduct of the accused. This rule specifically aims at protect-

---

76 Cassese, *supra* note 57, at 2.

77 For this topic, *see* MAY & WIERDA, *supra* note 43 at 727; KNOOPS, *supra* note 8, at 223–25 (2005).

78 *See also* Rule 92 *bis* of the RPE of the SCSL.

ing the rights of the accused by ensuring oral testimony when it concerns the heart of the prosecution case, and, as a result, it contributes to the prevention of miscarriages of justice. The Appeals Chamber of the ICTY, in *Prosecutor v. Galic*, interpreted Rule 92 *bis* as an exclusion of any written witness statement going to the proof of any act or conduct of the accused upon which the prosecution seeks to establish that the accused personally physically committed any of the crimes charged, that he planned, instigated, or ordered the crimes charged or that he was a superior to those who actually did commit the crimes. Moreover, proximity to the accused of the acts and conduct set out in the statement is relevant to a determination whether evidence should be admitted in written form at all.[79] The reason that written statements are not permissible to establish the criminal responsibility of an accused for acts and conduct of others is to prevent unfairness to the accused and to protect the criminal justice system. When this concept is applied to national criminal jurisdictions, it can serve as a procedural instrument to prevent miscarriages of justice. This observation is warranted given that Rule 92 *bis* (A)(i) requires, as an additional safeguard, that, for written evidence to be admitted, the evidence is cumulative, "in that other witnesses will give or have given oral testimony of similar facts." One of the central questions is whether the disallowance for the accused to cross-examine a prosecution witness on matters that do not go to the proof of his acts and conduct may risk a miscarriage of justice. In my opinion, this question can be answered in the affirmative both for civil law (in which judges have access to a complete "dossier") and common law jurisdictions (in which judges do not have a case file). Judge Patrick L. Robinson of the ICTY has eloquently set out the reasons why upholding this right to cross-examine may prevent unfairness and potential miscarriages of justice. In his article *Rough Edges in the Alignment of Legal Systems in the Proceedings of the ICTY*, he says that:

> The right of the accused to cross-examine prosecution witnesses—as recognized in Article 21(4)(e) of the Tribunal's Statute and Article 14(3)(e) of the International Covenant on Civil and Political Rights ("the ICCPR")—should be respected. It is a right

---

[79] *See* Prosecutor v. Galic, Case No. IT-98-29-AR 73.2, Appeals Chamber Decision on Interlocutory Appeal Concerning Rule 92 *bis* (c), June 7, 2002, paras. 9–12.

> that is personal to the accused, and it is the accused, who is better informed about his case than the Trial Chamber, who should determine whether cross-examination should take place. As the prosecution case progresses, so will the Trial Chamber's knowledge of the case for the accused, as it is revealed though cross-examination. However, this knowledge, even supplemented by information from the accused's opening address (if he has made one), will never match the knowledge that an accused has of his own case, which may only be fully revealed when he presents his defence. An accused should be allowed to cross-examine in respect of any item of evidence adduced by the prosecution on which it may rely to establish guilt. Although the witness statement does not go to proof of the acts and conduct of the accused, i.e., it is not evidence of an incident in which the accused was personally involved, or involved in any of the other ways set out in *Galic*, it may yet be of importance to the case of an accused who may wish to cross examine its maker to show that the incident did not take place at all, or for some other reason relevant to his case.[80]

In conclusion, were one to implement the notion that the accused should have the right to cross-examine the author of any statement that is part of the prosecution case against him, particularly when it goes to proof of his acts and conduct and ultimately his criminal responsibility, this could contribute to eradicating miscarriages of justice in international criminal cases.

D. CONTEMPORARY INTERNATIONAL LAW DEVELOPMENTS ON REDRESSING MISCARRIAGES OF JUSTICE

A last procedural mechanism *sui generis* can be found in General Assembly Resolution A/RES/60/147, *Basic Principles and Guidelines on the Right to a Remedy and Reparation for Victims of Gross Violations of International Human Rights Law and Serious Violations of International*

[80] *See* P.L. Robinson, *Rough Edges in the Alignment of Legal Systems in the Proceedings of the ICTY*, 3 JICJ 1043 (2005).

Humanitarian Law. With this Resolution, a new avenue within international law has been entered in that it formally affirms "the importance of addressing the question of remedies and reparation for victims of gross violations of international human rights law and serious violations of international humanitarian law in a systematic and thorough way at national and international levels."[81] Now that states are recommended to bring the principles enshrined by this Resolution to the attention of, among others, law enforcement officials, military and security forces and the judiciary, the impact thereof on the international criminal law systems of the world may be considerable.

The question arises whether this instrument and its principles also applies to the victims of miscarriages of justice in criminal cases, i.e., accused or convicted persons, subjected to wrongful convictions. To this end, paragraph 8 of the Resolution merits attention. This paragraph provides that "for the purposes of the present document, victims are persons who individually or collectively suffered harm, including physical or mental injury, emotional suffering, economic loss or substantial impairment of their fundamental rights, through acts or omissions that constitute gross violations of international human rights law, or serious violations of international humanitarian law."[82] It is tenable that the reference to "substantial impairment of their fundamental rights" also covers impairment resulting in miscarriages of justice due to serious violation of due process rights. This interpretation lends support from the Preamble to the Annex of this Resolution, containing the basic principles and guidelines in this regard. It emphasizes that victims of *crime and abuse of power* "have their right to access to justice and redress mechanisms fully respected." From this wording, "abuse of power" and "redress mechanisms," it is clear that this Resolution extends to accused persons who were or are subjected to miscarriage of justice. Read from this perspective, these Basic Principles and Guidelines of the GA Resolution

---

[81] See Preamble to General Assembly Resolution of Mar. 21, 2006, G.A. Res. A/Res/60/147 *Basic Principles and Guidelines on the Right to a Remedy and Reparation for Victims of Gross Violations of International Human Rights Law and Serious Violations of International Humanitarian Law*, *see*, for this topic, M. Cherif Bassiouni, Post Conflict Justice (2002).

[82] *See* G.A. Res. A/Res/60/147, art. 8.

comprise the following obligations for states to implement into their domestic legal systems:

(1) To adopt appropriate, effective legislative and administrative procedures and other appropriate measures that provide "fair, effective and prompt access to justice."[83] These guidelines may thus be interpreted as encompassing the obligation of states to prevent miscarriages of justice in criminal cases.

(2) To make available adequate, effective, prompt, and appropriate remedies. Also this obligation may be extended to the establishment of judicial proceedings to remedy miscarriages of justice.[84]

(3) In cases of gross violations of international human rights law (which may entail miscarriages of justice relative serious due process violations such as disclosure failures as regards exculpatory evidence), states are imbued with the duty to investigate.[85] This implies the duty of states to have all investigative means available to redress miscarriages of justice. The interpretation of the G.A. Resolution understood in this way, is reinforced by Article 24, providing that "victims . . . (of gross violations of international human rights law) should be entitled to seek and obtain information on the causes . . . and conditions pertaining to the gross violations of international human rights law . . . and to learn the truth in regard to these violations." This provision can thus serve as a legal foundation for defense counsel, dealing with petitions to redress miscarriages of justice in criminal cases, to seek disclosure and discovery of materials to remedy such miscarriages. The Drafters of this G.A. Resolution explicitly enumerate, among the reparation mechanisms in Section IX of the Resolution, that of "verification of the facts and full and public disclosure of the truth."[86] This reference seems self-evident and is also applicable to all information necessary to reverse a wrongful conviction.

---

83 *See id.*, art. 2(b).

84 *See id.*, arts. 2(c) and 3(d).

85 *See id.*, art. 4.

86 *See id.*, art. 22(b).

(4) Indirectly, the Resolution constitutes a significant acknowledgement of the need to promote international justice by having effective and adequate procedures in place to redress wrongful convictions.[87] This supports the notion set out in this book that these mechanisms are tantamount to *erga omnes* obligations.[88]

(5) Finally, the importance of the G.A. Resolution 60/147 to the phenomenon of miscarriages of justice in criminal cases lies in Article 19 dealing with "Restitution" of victims of gross violations of international human rights law. This provision says that restitution should, whenever possible, restore the victim "to the original situation before the gross violations. . . Restitution includes as appropriate: restoration of liberty." The latter form seems directly applicable to situations of miscarriages of justice.

Sequential to the issue of restitution, the Resolution addresses "satisfaction" as another reparation mechanism, including:

- an official declaration or a judicial decision restoring the dignity, the reputation and the rights of the victim; and
- public apology, including acknowledgement of the facts and acceptance of responsibility.[89]

It is thus to be hoped that states and international criminal tribunals will indeed construe their systems such that the contents of this Resolution, perceived in this way, will be respected and enforced.

---

87 *See id.*, art. 15.

88 *See* Chapters 1 and 12.

89 *See* G.A. Res. A/Res/60/147, art. 22(d) and (e).

CHAPTER 12

RECOMMENDATIONS AND FUTURE GUIDELINES AS TO THE PROTECTION AGAINST MISCARRIAGES OF JUSTICE

A. TOWARD A UNIFORM SYSTEM OF JUDICIAL SUPERVISION OF MISCARRIAGES OF JUSTICE

Based on the preceding chapter, this final chapter is dedicated to developing recommendations and guidelines for judges, prosecutor's, investigators, and defense lawyers that may be instrumental in preventing miscarriages of justice.

1. Disclosure as Principal Procedural Remedy

The case of *R. v. Ward*[1] sets forth several disclosure principles that are of perennial concern in the prevention or redressing of miscarriages of justice. These principles can serve as a summary and as guidelines for defense counsel confronted with retrial proceedings.

First, government forensic scientists are under a clear duty to act impartially in the course of criminal investigations. The prosecution is obliged to make available to the defense any witness whom they did not propose to call but whom they knew could give material evidence and any evidence that tended either to weaken the prosecution case or strengthen the defense case. The prosecution also has a positive duty, independent of the duties imposed by the Crown Court (Advance Notice of Expert Evidence) Rules 1987, to disclose any scientific evidence that might arguably assist the defense. There is a clear obligation on an expert witness to disclose evidence of any tests or experiments that he had car-

[1] For this case, *see* Chapter 4.

ried out or had knowledge of which tended to cast doubt on an opinion he was expressing, and to bring the records of any such tests or other party. In the *Ward* case, there had been a failure by the government scientists who had given evidence at the appellant's trial, by some members of the police force investigating the offences, and by some of the staff of the Director of Public Prosecutions and counsel advising them, to comply with the duty of disclosure, which had resulted in a grave miscarriage of justice, and the appeal was allowed on those grounds.

Second, expert medical evidence of a psychiatrist or psychologist that a defendant, while not suffering from mental illness, was suffering from a personality disorder so serious as to be properly described as a mental disorder, might be admissible to demonstrate the unreliability of admission or confessions made by that defendant, although such evidence might only be admitted on rare occasions. After considering fresh medical evidence, and medical evidence that had been in existence at the time of the appellant's trial but that had not been disclosed, the Court in the *Ward* case was not satisfied that the truth of the appellant's admissions and confessions could be relied on, and on that ground also her conviction was quashed.

Third, if the prosecution wish to claim public interest immunity in a criminal trial for documents that might help the defense case, they must give notice of their intentions to the defense so that, if necessary, the court could be asked to rule on the question. If, in a wholly exceptional case, the prosecution was not prepared for the issue to be decided by the court, the prosecution would, inevitably, have to be abandoned.

2. Future Protection Against Miscarriages of Justice: Enhancing Judicial Supervision of Prosecutorial Conduct

In the context of miscarriages of justice this study has shown that one of the main causes of such miscarriages lies within the failure of the prosecution to properly disclose exculpatory evidence or investigate this evidence. The question arises how such failures could be prevented in future cases. In this context, the following recommendation can be developed.

A mechanism within U.S. case law relates to the issuance of disciplinary proceedings against a prosecutor for failing to disclose "evidence or information known to the prosecutor that tends to negate the guilt of the accused or mitigates the offence, and, in connection with sentencing, disclose to the defence and to the tribunal all unprivileged mitigating information known to the prosecutor."[2] A case involving this mechanism took place before the Supreme Court of Louisiana *in re Roger W. Jordan, Jr.*, in which a former Orleans Parish prosecutor was formally charged, alleging that he violated Rules 3.8(d)(2) and 8.4(a)(3) of the *Rules of Professional Conduct* by failing to timely disclose to the defense evidence tending to negate the guilt of the accused or mitigate the offense. The formal charges against respondent arose from the capital prosecution of Shareef Cousin and respondent's undisputed failure to turn over an eyewitness's statement to the defense. Several days after the completion of the guilt phase of the trial, but before the penalty phase, a copy of an exculpatory statement, a second statement of the witness, Babin, was delivered anonymously to defense counsel. On appeal, the defense raised as error respondent's failure to produce the exculpatory statement prior to trial. This Court did not reach that issue. Instead, a unanimous Court reversed Cousin's conviction and death sentence based on the erroneous admission of a witness's testimony as impeachment evidence and respondent's improper use of that evidence in closing argument. The Court commented in footnotes that Babin's second statement was "obviously" exculpatory, material to the issue of guilt, and "clearly" should have been produced to the defense under *Brady* and *Kyles v. Whitley*.[3] Interestingly, the Supreme Court of Louisiana noted that it never before had been confronted with such a matter.[4]

Faced with the charge against Prosecutor Jordan, the Supreme Court of Louisiana, in the judgment of June 29, 2005,[5] enunciated the following guidelines and observations important to the prevention of miscarriages of justice:

---

2 *See* U.S. RULES OF PROFESSIONAL CONDUCT, Rule 3.8(d).

3 *See* 514 U.S.419, 115 S. Ct. 1555, 131 L. Ed. 2d 490 (1995)

4 For the underlying case, *see* State v. Cousin, 710 So. 2d 1065, 1066 and 1073 (La. 1998).

5 No. 2004-B-2397.

(1) In our system of justice, we entrust vast discretion to a prosecutor. *In re Toups*, 2000–0634 p. 10 (La. 11/28/00), 773 So.2d 709, 715. Because a prosecutor is given such great power and discretion, he is also charged with a high ethical standard.

(2) A prosecutor is entrusted with upholding the integrity of the criminal justice system by ensuring that justice is served for both the victims of crimes and the accused. "Society wins not only when the guilty are convicted but when criminal trials are fair; our system of the administration of justice suffers when any accused is treated unfairly."[6]

(3) The actions, or inactions in this case, of the prosecutor are paramount to a fair administration of justice; and the people of this state must have confidence in a prosecutor's integrity in performing his duty to disclose exculpatory evidence in order for the system to be just. Any intentional deviation from the principle of the fair administration of justice will be dealt with harshly by a judge as the Supreme Court noted.

(4) Furthermore the Supreme Court said that the duty of a prosecutor to disclose exculpatory evidence is embedded in the principle that a criminal defendant is deprived of a fair trial when the state withholds exculpatory evidence that is material to guilt or punishment. The state's failure to disclose material evidence favorable to a criminal defendant implicates more than the defendant's discovery rights; the prosecutor has an affirmative duty to disclose such evidence under the Fourteenth Amendment's Due Process Clause. Failure to reveal this evidence implicates the defendant's right to a fair trial.[7]

(5) As to the question whether the questioned evidence is material under *Brady*, the Supreme Court referred to its ruling in the *Marshall* case, 94-0461 p. 16 (La. 9/5/95), 660 So.2d

[6] Brady v. Maryland, 373 U.S. 83, 87 (1963).

[7] United States v. Agurs, 427 U.S. 97, 96 S. Ct. 2392, 49 L. Ed. 2d 342 (1976); State v. Marshall, 660 So. 2d 819, 825 (La. 1995).

819, 826: The issue is whether the exculpatory evidence is material under the Brady-Bagley-Kyles line of cases. Evidence is material only if it is reasonably probable that the result of the proceeding would have been different had the evidence been disclosed to the defense. A reasonable probability is one which is sufficient to undermine confidence in the outcome.[8] This Court must provide a cumulative evaluation of the suppressed evidence, keeping in mind that *Marshall* does not have to show that, with the addition of the suppressed evidence, his trial would have resulted in acquittal or that there would be an insufficiency of the evidence to support a conviction. *Marshall* need only show that "disclosure of the suppressed evidence to competent counsel would have made a different result reasonably probable."[9]

(6) In this regard the Supreme Court observed that during his testimony before the hearing committee, Mr. Jordan testified that he did not believe Ms. Babin's second statement was material and did not qualify as the type of evidence to be disclosed under *Brady*. Specifically, Mr. Jordan stated that he thought the evidence was inculpatory rather than exculpatory as Ms. Babin recounted specific details regarding the defendant's clothing and colorful socks.

(7) The Supreme Court held however that, while the definition of materiality set forth in *Kyles* and its progeny may be seen as leaving a prosecutor with a degree of discretion, it does not. *Kyles*, 514 U.S. at 438.

(8) According to the Supreme Court, exculpatory evidence includes evidence which impeaches the testimony of a witness whose credibility or reliability may determine guilt or innocence. *Giglio v. United States*, 405 U.S. 150, 92 S.Ct. 763, 31 L.Ed. 104 (1972). Additionally, *United States v. Bagley*, 473 U.S. 667, 676, 105 S.Ct. 3375, 3380, 87 L.Ed.2d 481 (1985), reiterates the principle that there is no distinc-

---

8 United States v. Bagley, 473 U.S. 667, 682 (1985).

9 Kyles v. Whitley, 514 U.S. 419, 440 (1995).

tion between exculpatory evidence and impeachment evidence under *Brady*. In this case, the Supreme Court held that Ms. Babin's second statement negates her ability to positively identify the defendant in a line-up. The statement should have been disclosed to the defense.[10]

(9) Interestingly the Supreme Court in the *Cousin* case held that a prosecutor anxious about "tacking too close to the wind will disclose a favorable piece of evidence" and "will resolve doubtful questions in favour of disclosure."[11] Mr. Jordan failed to produce evidence which was clearly exculpatory and should have resolved this issue in favour of disclosure and therefore violated Rule 3.8(d) by failing to disclose the second statement of Ms. Babin to the defendant.

The conclusions drawn by the Supreme Court of Louisiana could also apply to other cases and other legal systems in order to serve as an incentive to prosecutors to strictly comply with disclosure obligations in order to prevent miscarriages of justice.[12] One could say that prosecutors are supposed to be capable of rising above their role as advocate to ensure that justice is done.[13]

3. Proper and Timely Engagement of Expert Witnesses

Another mechanism and recommendation to prevent or redress wrongful convictions, i.e., miscarriages of justice, is the invocation of expert witness testimony in a wide array of disciplines already within criminal investigations to supervise the investigative actions of the police and/or prosecution.

Expert witness testimony, particularly social and psychological science expert witness testimony, seems to have become a prerequisite in disputed confession cases now that both the inquisitorial and adversar-

---

10 *See* State v. Cousin, 710 So. 2d 1065 (La. 1998).

11 *See id.*, at 1073, n.8.

12 *See also*, in this regard, the opinion of Justice Sandra Day O'Connor in *Herrera v. Collins*, 506 U.S. 390, 113 S. Ct. 853, 122 L. Ed. 2d 203 (1993).

13 *See* Berger v. United States, 295 U.S. 78 (1935).

ial criminal law systems cannot preclude the conviction of innocent persons based on unreliable and false confessions.[14] As observed in this book, police-induced false confessions have been among the primary causes of miscarriages of justice.[15] In particular, two reasons emerge as to why expert witness testimony can prevent or redress false confessions leading to miscarriages of justice:

(1) Expert witness testimony on this topic may assist a trial chamber, i.e., triers of fact, in assessing the psychological principles, practices, and processes of contemporary (police) interrogation methods, thus enabling the judges to distinguish reliable confessions from unreliable ones.[16] Under common law systems, expert witness testimony on the reliability of confessions may assist the pre-trial judge in deciding whether a confession should be admissible at trial. Specifically, expert witness testimony can inform the judiciary as to whether and why certain interrogation methods are seen as coercive and eligible to break the will of the accused.[17] The suppression of false confessions, as early as possible in the pre-trial proceedings, could potentially reduce the instances of miscarriages of justice.

(2) The invocation of expert witness testimony in the suppression of false confessions can also have a preventive effect in that judges, prosecutors, and police officers will be more aware that confessions can be false. Indeed, by revealing false confessions in interrogation methods, particularly in cases that rest solely or to a decisive extent on disputed confessions, expert witnesses in this area may deter police from applying coercive interrogation methods and improve police and prosecutorial (ethical) behavior *vis-à-vis* statements of an accused.[18]

---

[14] *See* Richard A. Leo, *False Confessions: Causes, Consequences and Solutions*, *in* WRONGFULLY CONVICTED: PERSPECTIVES ON FAILED JUSTICE 50 (Saundra D. Westervelt & John A. Humphrey eds., 2001).

[15] *Id.* at 44–45.

[16] *Id.*

[17] *Id.* at 51.

[18] *Id.* at 52.

Expert witness testimony is of relevance in DNA cases, particularly to ensure contra-expertise.

4. Minimizing the Inherent Risks in Forensic Evidence: Proactive Tasks for Defense Lawyers

As seen in Chapter 8, the U.S. Supreme Court in *Daubert v. Merrell Dow Pharmaceuticals Inc.* (1993) requires a reliability assessment for forensic expert testimony to be admitted, if challenged.[19] As a result, defense lawyers can proactively be engaged in:

(1) Reducing the occurrence of erroneous forensic science results by adequately, timely, and adamantly calling for a thorough reliability test in contentious cases.[20]

(2) Reducing such occurrence by timely requesting the laboratory data, such as the complete DNA profiles in a certain case, which underlie a particular test result, in order to obtain a counter-expertise or independent review. Retesting of disputed laboratory data and subjecting them to review should be at the basis of the criminal defense engagement in cases that rely heavily on forensic evidence.[21]

5. Statutory Obligation as to Recording Police Interviews

Another mechanism as to the prevention or rectification of miscarriages of justice involves the promulgation of a (statutory) mandatory obligation to electronically record all police interviews in their entirety. Three reasons emerge that justify this observation and recommendation.

---

19 *See* George Castelle & Elizabeth Loftus, *Misinformation and Wrongful Convictions, in* WRONGFULLY CONVICTED: PERSPECTIVES ON FAILED JUSTICE 28 (Saundra D. Westervelt & John A Humphrey eds., 2001).

20 *Id.; see also* for the requirement that requests for counter-expertise will be submitted timely during the criminal proceedings, Judgment Dutch Supreme Court, Nov. 22, 2005, Case No. 3527.04, rejecting a defense request to obtain DNA profiles when the defense failed to proactively engage counter-expertise.

21 *See* Castelle & Loftus, *supra* note 19.

(1) As noted by other scholars, videotaping of police interviews ensures an objective and reviewable record of the application of police interrogation methods.[22] In civil law systems, such an obligation particularly arises in view of the fact that statements of defendants and witnesses are often summarized rather than taken verbatim. In order to assess the credibility of these statements, judges must rely on a considerable level of subjectivity, depending on the way the police officers have summarized the statements in question.

(2) Electronic recording of police interviews forms an incentive that police officials will refrain from abusive and coercive interrogation techniques, especially when the electronic record of the interview becomes part of the disclosure obligations of the prosecution.[23]

(3) Such recording may also increase the integrity and quality of the criminal trials and enhance the trust of accused individuals in the criminal justice system. Moreover, such mandatory videotaping may lead to a higher level of trust for accuseds to adduce statements to the police.

6. Improvement in Police Training and Awareness

Improvement of police training and, consequently, the endorsement of an awareness on the part of police, prosecutorial and judicial authorities would be of great value in this regard. In general, police officers are not specifically trained to analyze the psychology of an interrogation and the processes leading to a confession.[24] This training should comprise the following elements:

(1) Dissemination to the police, relative to the causes and factors that provoke police-induced false confessions, including the different types of false confessions that may arise.[25]

---

22 *See* Leo, *supra* note 14, at 49.

23 *Id.* at 50.

24 *Id.* at 48.

25 *Id.* at 48.

Only then can police detectives learn and be made aware of how to prevent a potential miscarriage of justice based on false confessions. Conversely, they are alerted as to how to obtain trustworthy confessions and evidence.

(2) Such training should focus on how to verify an accused's admission of guilt in that the police detectives should be able to determine whether a confession reveals any "guilty knowledge" (i.e., knowledge that is known only to the true perpetrator of the crime and is not disclosed early by police) and whether it is corroborated by objective supporting evidence, such as physical or medical evidence.[26]

(3) Circumspection as to interrogations of mentally retarded accused's as set forth in Chapter 5.

Importantly, police detectives should be educated that their criminal investigations should not be led by self-validating assumptions of the accused's guilt and their potentially biased position *vis-à-vis* the accused or a theory of the criminal case. Rather, they should be trained and made aware that one of the fundamental ways of preventing miscarriages of justice is to treat and approach each criminal investigation as a neutral hypothesis, which is to be objectively tested in view of all the relevant facts of the case, and should be open to more than one scenario.[27]

7. Refining the Laws on Review of International Criminal Cases: A Uniform Provision

The last conclusion and recommendation pertains to the promulgation of a uniform and justifiable review test in international criminal cases. In this regard, the "real possibility" test, as enshrined by the British CCRC, could serve as such a uniform standard. As shown in Chapter 7, this test departs from strict legal requirements; rather it relies on principles of reasonableness.

---

26 *Id.* at 48–49.

27 *Id.* at 48–49. For this situation, *see also* the landmark Dutch criminal case titled the *Puttense Homicide* case, which was reopened by the Dutch Supreme Court on April 26, 2001; *see* Chapter 7.

Within this approach, a changed opinion of an expert witness or new expert evidence can result in a retrial, presupposing that this evidence is solid, and the accused cannot reasonably be blamed for not producing this evidence at trial.[28]

In this connection, the following uniform review provision, influenced by Article 84(1)(a) of the ICC Statute, could be considered in both civil law as well as common law systems, when a question arises as to whether and when new expert evidence can warrant the reopening of a criminal case. In this uniform provision, review of a conviction can be requested when new forensic evidence emerges that is incompatible with the initial conviction. This criterion may be met in the event:

(1) It is made probable that this initial conviction is henceforth no longer "safe"; and

(2) The court was unaware of said new forensic evidence, while it is probable that such unawareness can reasonably not be attributed to the accused.[29]

This provision also incorporates the uniform disclosure standard as formulated in the U.S. Supreme Court in the *Bagley* case.[30] Interestingly, Article 84(1)(a) of the ICC Statute opens the possibility for review of ICC judgments on the basis of new facts or evidence that was not available at trial, while it is probable that such materials "would have been likely to have resulted in a different verdict," and the accused cannot be blamed for this non-availability.[31]

On the basis of the conclusions set forth in this book, the proposed provision is not only in keeping with international criminal law standards, but also reflects the principles of this research. This provision could be combined with a judicially independent system to review criminal cases modelled on the example of the British CCRC.[32]

---

28 *See* G.G.J. Knoops, *De Puttense Moordzaak*, 29 DUTCH LEG. J. NJB 1402–07 (2003); *see also* thesis Niels van Schaik, *De interpretatie van het strafrechtelijk novumbegrip door de Hoge Raad*, University of Utrecht, 87 (2006).

29 *See*, for this proposal, Knoops, *supra* note 28, at 1407.

30 For this case, *see* Chapters 4 and 7.

31 *See also* Chapter 7.

32 *Id.*

B. CONCLUDING RECOMMENDATION: THE PROTECTION AGAINST MISCARRIAGES OF JUSTICE AS AN *ERGA OMNES* OBLIGATION

In the end, it seems fair to conclude that the key to the protection against miscarriages of justice, in both international and national criminal cases, lies in the applicability of the concept of responsibility to individuals subjected to criminal prosecutions. As long as this form of legal protection is not perceived and qualified as being part of states' *erga omnes* obligations under international law, with a direct effect on national jurisdictions, miscarriages of justice can never be effectively redressed.

TABLE OF AUTHORITIES

BASSIOUNI, M. CHERIF, POST-CONFLICT JUSTICE (2002).

Cassese, Antonio, *Effective Remedies for Abuse of Process in General International Law, Treaty Law and the Russian Legal System*, unpublished paper (2004).

Castelle, George & Elizabeth Loftus, *Misinformation and Wrongful Convictions, in* WRONGLY CONVICTED: PERSPECTIVES ON FAILED JUSTICE 26 (Saundra D. Westervelt & John A. Humphrey, eds., 2001).

CONNORS, EDWARD, THOMAS LUNDREGAN, NEAL MILLER & TOM MCEWAN, CONVICTED BY JURIES, EXONERATED BY SCIENCE: CASE STUDIES IN THE USE OF DNA EVIDENCE TO ESTABLISH INNOCENCE AFTER TRIAL, Washington D.C., National Institute of Justice, 1996.

CRAWFORD, JAMES, THE INTERNATIONAL LAW COMMISSION'S ARTICLES ON STATE RESPONSIBILITY 77 (2002).

de Bertodano, Sylvia, *Current Developments in Internationalized Courts*, 1 JICJ 244 (2003).

FONTHAM, MICHAEL R., TRIAL TECHNIQUE AND EVIDENCE (2002).

Freckleton, Ian, *A Taxonomy of Error and Deviance, in* HARMONISATION IN FORENSIC EXPERTISE 319–320 (J.F. Nijboer & W.J.J.M. Sprangers eds., 2000).

GUDJONSSON, G.H., THE PSYCHOLOGY OF INTERROGATIONS, CONFESSIONS AND TESTIMONY (1993).

GUDJONSSON, G.H., THE PSYCHOLOGY OF INTERROGATIONS AND CONFESSIONS: A HANDBOOK (2003).

Holmes, William M., *Who are the Wrongly Convicted on Death Row?, in* WRONGLY CONVICTED: PERSPECTIVES ON FAILED JUSTICE 101 (Saundra D. Westervelt & John A. Humphrey eds., 2001).

Horselenberg, Robert & Ton Smeets, *False Confessions*, 14 ADVOCATENBLAD (Journal for the Dutch Bar Association) 623 (2005).

Jobling, Mark A. & Peter Gill, *Encoded Evidence: DNA in Forensic Analysis*, 5 NATURE REVIEWS GENETICS 739 (2004).

Kassin, S.M., *On the Psychology of Confessions: Does Innocence Put Innocents at Risk?*, 2 AM. PSYCHOLOGIST 215–28 (2005).

Kassin, Saul M. & Gisli H. Gudjonsson, *The Psychology of Confession: A Review of the Literature and Issues*, 2 PSYCHOL. SCI. 56 (2004).

Kassin, S.M. & K.L. Kiechel, *The Social Psychology of False Confessions: Compliance, Internalization and Confabulation*, 7 PSYCHOL. SCI. 125–28 (1996).

Kaul, Hans-Peter, *Construction Site for More Justice: The International Criminal Court after Two Years*, 2 AIIL 3715–29 (2005).

Kloosterman, Ate D. & Paula Kersbergen, *Efficacy and Limits of Genotyping Low Copy Number (LCN) DNA Samples by Multiplex PCR of STR Loci*, unpublished.

Knoops, G.G.J., *De Puttense Moordzaak*, 29 NEDERLANDS JURISTENBLAD 1402–07 (2002).

KNOOPS, G.J., DEFENSES IN CONTEMPORARY INTERNATIONAL CRIMINAL LAW (2001).

KNOOPS, G.J., SURRENDERING TO INTERNATIONAL CRIMINAL TRIBUNALS: CONTEMPORARY PRACTICE AND PROCEDURES (2002).

KNOOPS, G.J., THEORY AND PRACTICE OF INTERNATIONAL AND INTERNATIONALIZED CRIMINAL PROCEEDINGS (2005).

Leahy, Patrick, *The Innocence Protection Act of 2001*, 29 HOFSTRA L. REV. 1113–54 (2001).

Leo, Richard A., *False Confessions: Causes, Consequences and Solutions, in* WRONGFULLY CONVICTED: PERSPECTIVES ON FAILED JUSTICE 50 (Saundra D. Westervelt & John A. Humphrey eds., 2001).

Martin, Dianne L., *The Police Role in Wrongful Convictions: An International Comparative Study, in* WRONGLY CONVICTED: PERSPECTIVES ON FAILED JUSTICE 77–95 (Saundra D. Westervelt & John A. Humphrey eds., 2001).

MAUET, THOMAS A., FUNDAMENTALS OF TRIAL TECHNIQUES (1992).

MAY, RICHARD & MARIEKE WIERDA, INTERNATIONAL CRIMINAL EVIDENCE (2002).

McCloskey, James, *Convicting the Innocent*, 2 CRIMINAL JUSTICE ETHICS 54–59 (1989).

Middlemiss, Jim, *Guilty Until Proven Innocent*, 3 CANADIAN LAW. 20–25 (1991).

Mundis, Daryl A., *From Common Law Towards Civil Law: The Evolution of the ICTY Rules of Procedure and Evidence*, 2 LEIDEN J. INT'L L. 367–82 (2001).

Radelet, Michael L., *Foreword, in* WRONGLY CONVICTED: PERSPECTIVES ON FAILED JUSTICE xi (Saundra D. Westervelt & John A. Humphrey eds., 2001).

RAGAZZI, M., THE CONCEPT OF INTERNATIONAL OBLIGATIONS *ERGA OMNES* (1997).

Robinson, P.L., *Rough Edges in the Alignment of Legal Systems in the Proceedings of the ICTY*, 3 JICJ 1043 (2005).

SCHABAS, WILLIAM, A., AN INTRODUCTION TO THE INTERNATIONAL CRIMINAL COURT (2001).

SCHABAS, WILLIAM A., THE ABOLITION OF THE DEATH PENALTY IN INTERNATIONAL LAW (2002).

Scheck, Barry & Peter Neufeld, *DNA and Innocence Scholarship, in* WRONGLY CONVICTED: PERSPECTIVES ON FAILED JUSTICE 241 (Saundra D. Westervelt & John A. Humphrey eds., 2001).

Spencer, John R., *Evidence and Forensic Science, in* HARMONISATION IN FORENSIC EXPERTISE 551 (J.F. Nijboer & W.J.J.M. Sprangers eds., 2000).

van Kampen, Petra, *Confronting Expert Evidence under the European Conventions, in* HARMONISATION IN FORENSIC EXPERTISE 201 (J.F. Nijboer & W.J.J.M. Sprangers eds., 2000).

Whitaker, J.P., E.A. Cotton & P. Gill, *A Comparison of the Characteristics of Profiles Produced with the AMPF1STR SGM Plus TM Multiplex System for Both Standard and Low Copy Number (LCN) STR DNA Analysis,* 123 FORENSIC SCI. INT'L 215 (2001).

TABLE OF CASES

Canada

ECHR

Human Rights Committee

Inter-American Commission on Human Rights

International Court of Justice (ICJ)

ICTR

ICTY

United States

INDEX